T0152441

MINNESOTA
ADVENTURE WEEKENDS
Your Guide to the Best Outdoor Getaways

Jeff Moravec

MENASHA RIDGE PRESS
Your Guide to the Outdoors Since 1982
an imprint of AdventureKEEN

MINNESOTA ADVENTURE WEEKENDS

Copyright © 2019 by Jeff Moravec
All rights reserved
Published by Menasha Ridge Press
Distributed by Publishers Group West
Manufactured in the United States of America
First edition, fourth printing 2024

Cover and interior design: Jonathan Norberg
Interior photographs: Jeff Moravec
Cover photographs: *Front:* welcomia/Shutterstock; *back:* yurt at Glendalough State Park, Jeff Moravec
Cartography: Steve Jones
Typography: Monica Ahlman
Indexer: Joanna E. Sprott

Library of Congress Cataloging-in-Publication Data
Names: Moravec, Jeff, 1955– author.
Title: Minnesota adventure weekends : Your guide to the best outdoor getaways / Jeff Moravec.
Description: First edition. | Birmingham, AL : Menasha Ridge Press, [2019] |
    Includes bibliographical references and index.
Identifiers: LCCN 2018054265| ISBN 9781634041560 (pbk.) | ISBN 9781634041577 (ebk.)
Subjects: LCSH: Outdoor recreation—Minnesota—Guidebooks. |
    Recreation areas—Minnesota—Guidebooks. | Hiking—Minnesota—Guidebooks. |
    Minnesota—Guidebooks.
Classification: LCC GV54.M6 M67 2019 | DDC 790.09776—dc23
LC record available at https://lccn.loc.gov/2018054265

MENASHA RIDGE PRESS
An imprint of AdventureKEEN
2204 First Ave. S., Suite 102
Birmingham, AL 35233
800-678-7006, fax 877-374-9016

Visit menasharidge.com for a complete listing of our books and for ordering information. Contact us at our website, at facebook.com/menasharidge, or at twitter.com/menasharidge with questions or comments. To find out more about who we are and what we're doing, visit blog.menasharidge.com.

SAFETY NOTICE: Although Menasha Ridge Press and the author have made every attempt to ensure that the information in this book is accurate at press time, they are not responsible for any loss, damage, injury, or inconvenience that may occur to anyone while using this book. You are responsible for your own safety and health while following the adventures described here. Always check local conditions, know your limitations, and consult a map.

DEDICATION

To my wife, Kelly, for sharing my love of the outdoors, and for always understanding and supporting my wanderlust.

ACKNOWLEDGMENTS

A fellow wordsmith once told me that if you knew what it was going to take to complete a book, you'd never start it. He was probably right. But researching and writing this book was a labor of love, and I'm thankful for the opportunity.

I would like to thank my wife, Kelly; daughter, Allyson; and son, Zach. It wasn't until we became a family that my interest in the outdoors grew into a lifetime joy. While I've spent countless hours in the woods by myself, it was—and is—our family excursions that truly warm my soul. Instilling an appreciation for the outdoors in my children, I believe, will be the accomplishment of my lifetime. To see my daughter's true elation at discovering the backpacking trails of Isle Royale in 2014 was a moment I'll remember forever. It made the leaking tents, heel blisters, and mosquito bites over the years all worthwhile.

I also want to thank Bob Timmons, my editor at the Outdoors Weekend section of Minneapolis's *Star Tribune*. While I've been a writer my entire life, I'd never really written about the outdoors until Bob gave me a chance. Without his encouragement and support of my newspaper writing, I would never have had the opportunity to be involved in this project. Bob's a great editor and a good guy.

Thanks to Tim Jackson at AdventureKEEN for giving me the chance to write this book, although I would have finished a lot faster if he hadn't always been engaging me in conversation about Jason Isbell and college football. Tim and the entire team at AdventureKEEN have been a pleasure to work with.

Thanks must also go to all the people in Minnesota, professionals and volunteers, who work so hard to keep our natural resources pristine. A special shout-out goes to Jo Swanson and everyone at the Superior Hiking Trail Association. I'm especially thankful for the folks at the state parks, who are overworked and underpaid but do their jobs so well. They are a friendly, helpful lot, and their dedication is amazing.

I'm also grateful to Alison Heebsh. Thanks for thinking of me.

And finally, thanks to my brother, Steve, and to Jim Atkins. You inspired me more than you knew, and I wish you were here to see this book.

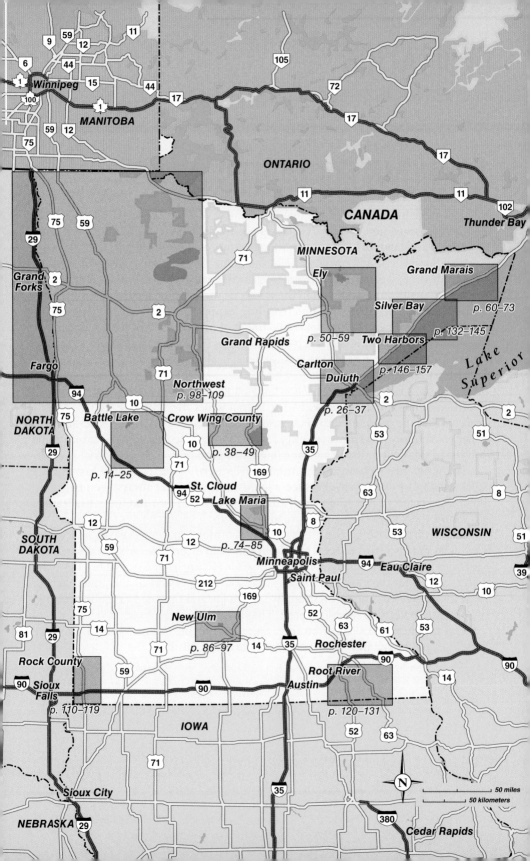

TABLE OF CONTENTS

PREFACE

While I may have difficulty remembering what I had for lunch yesterday, I very clearly recall the moment a quarter century ago when my love affair with the Minnesota outdoors began.

It was my first visit to North Shore of Lake Superior, and I was intrigued with the signs I was seeing pointing toward the Superior Hiking Trail. I pulled my car over by one of the markers at a wayside rest and scrambled up a hill to the start of the hiking path. I peeked down the trail, then ventured a few steps in. Aspen, birch, and white cedar shaded the track as I was drawn into the forest. I left the woods a few hours later, but the woods never left me.

In the 25 years since that day, as my kids grew into adulthood, I've crisscrossed Minnesota more times than I can count, solo and with the family. Our vacations were never at Disneyland (sorry, kids) but in the state parks and the Boundary Waters Canoe Area and on backpacking trails. We've logged nearly 500 nights in tents (yes, I keep track). We've watched moose feeding in ponds, discovered fresh bear tracks in our campsite, and had gray jays snatch popcorn from our picnic table. We've fought whitecaps while paddling through the wilderness and kayaked Superior on days when it was like glass. I've worn out more sleeping bags than I can count.

It has been heaven (except for a few of those teeth-rattling 3 a.m. thunderstorms) and a pleasure watching my kids as adults take off on their own outdoor adventures. Over the years, as any of my friends or family will tell you, it takes little for me to

Forest above Lake Superior

proselytize about the wonders of the Minnesota outdoors. So it's a privilege to share with those of you reading this book a few of the places we've grown to know and love.

Often, as a young family with busy schedules, we had to make the most of our time outdoors, and we learned how to pack as much as we could into a weekend. The outdoors is about recharging and soaking in nature, of course, so at the same time we were always careful to try to find a happy medium that wouldn't make the weekend feel like work. My goal has been to duplicate that vibe in this book. But whether you simply stare at a campfire (and I've done plenty of that) or sweat your way through a 30-mile bike ride, the important thing is that you're in the fresh air.

■ Hauling firewood at Lake Maria State Park

This is, of course, a guidebook. It's meant to help you figure out where you want to visit and what you want to do while you're there. But I'm conscious (maybe overly so) of the impact that social media has on us these days. Far too many people heading to the outdoors don't feel comfortable stepping outside unless their Facebook friends have recommended a minute-to-minute itinerary and told them what to expect and what they'll see on every step of their journey. Let's keep some of the exploration in exploration! I've tried to give you a good sense of the places in this book without robbing you of the enjoyment of discovering on your own what these locations have to offer. So please use this book as a guide, not the gospel.

Wherever your journeys in Minnesota take you, I hope your travels inspire you the way mine have inspired me.

—*Jeff Moravec*

MINNESOTA ADVENTURE ACCOLADES

BEST FOR WHITEWATER PADDLING
Carlton (page 26)

BEST FOR FLATWATER PADDLING
Crow Wing County (page 38)

Root River (page 120)

Two Harbors (page 146)

BEST FOR HIKING
Grand Marais (page 60)

Silver Bay (page 132)

Two Harbors (page 146)

BEST FOR MOUNTAIN BIKERS
Crow Wing County (page 38)

Grand Marais (page 60)

BEST FOR ROAD CYCLISTS
Battle Lake (page 14)

Root River (page 120)

Two Harbors (page 146)

BEST FOR CLIMBERS
Rock County (page 110)

Silver Bay (page 132)

BEST FOR KIDS
Ely (page 50)

New Ulm (page 86)

Root River (page 120)

Two Harbors (page 146)

BEST FOR NEW ADVENTURERS
Lake Maria (page 74)

Root River (page 120)

Grand Marais (page 60)

BEST FOR SOLITUDE
Battle Lake (page 14)

Rock County (page 110)

Lake Maria (page 74)

■ Palisade Head at Tettegouche State Park

INTRODUCTION

In one of the chapters of this book, I put forth the argument that the topography of Minnesota is as diverse as anywhere (or almost anywhere) in the country. I don't know if that's truth or just opinion. Maybe people in most states think the same about their home as I do mine. But I do know that anyone who travels around Minnesota is going to find an incredible diversity of geographic features.

You probably know all about our 10,000 lakes, of course—even though last time anyone checked there were actually 11,832 of them. More than 1,100 of those lakes (and countless rivers and streams) are in the **Boundary Waters Canoe Area,** one of the nation's premier destinations for wilderness paddling. When it comes to captivating people, one river in the state—**the Mississippi**—has as much cache as the lakes, in large part because you can actually step over it where it begins as a trickle in Itasca State Park. And, finally, when it comes to water, Minnesota borders about 150 miles of **Lake Superior,** the largest freshwater lake in the world by surface area.

But it's not all about the water, and that's one of the things you'll discover quickly as you travel around Minnesota on weekend adventures.

In the southeastern corner of the state is the **Driftless Area,** which essentially refers to land that was never squashed by the glaciers. The region is dominated by magnificent bluffs and river valleys, with scenery that stuns visitors and is unlike anywhere else in Minnesota.

If you move west to the southwestern border, you'll run into prairie grasslands such as those that surround **Blue Mounds State Park** near Luverne. It's part of only 4% of what's left of the 170 million acres of prairie that once dominated much of

North America, and a walk through the tall grass will make you feel like you've traveled through time.

In between, and spreading toward the northern part of the state, are the **Big Woods**, hardwood forests dominated by magnificent oak, sugar maple, basswood, and ash trees. While these woods once covered nearly 5,000 square miles in Minnesota and neighboring states, development erased most of the old forest; fortunately, in state parks such as **Lake Maria** and **Nerstrand Big Woods**, they remain as they were 150 years ago.

There are also the boreal coniferous forests of northern Minnesota, a treasure to Boundary Waters paddlers as well as the hikers who traverse the 310-mile **Superior Hiking Trail** through the Sawtooth Mountains than run along Lake Superior.

But this isn't a geography lesson, so I will limit myself to the highlights and apologize for other areas I've left out. The point here is to highlight the diversity of the state and to emphasize that that diversity would not exist were it not for all the efforts made for so many years to preserve Minnesota's lands in their natural state, ready-made for recreation.

Outdoor recreation is near and dear to the hearts of Minnesotans, and that is reflected best in our state park system. While the parks sometimes struggle with budgetary issues, I think you'd be hard-pressed to find another state with a system as good as this one. And, with all due respect, I wish national park campgrounds were half as good as the ones you'll find in Minnesota.

The system is quantity as well as quality—at last count, 67 state parks, nine recreation areas, more than 1,300 miles of state trails and 4,500 miles of water trails, as well as 62 state forest campgrounds and day-use areas. There are also some 18 parcels of land, many of which include campgrounds, administered by the U.S. Forest Service, mostly in the northern part of the state.

In short, your issue is not going to be difficulty finding a spot that suits you for an adventure weekend in Minnesota; it's going to be finding the time to visit them all. So there's only one thing to do. Get started, and have fun.

■ St. Louis River near Carlton

HOW TO USE THIS BOOK

This book introduces you to some of the best outdoor recreation options around the state of Minnesota, keeping in mind that you only have a weekend—48 hours—to explore a destination. Each location was chosen because it offers easily accessible outdoor fun and minimal travel time in between activities, and I've attempted to include locations that emphasize different activities (one may have more biking trails, while another could offer extensive hiking opportunities). Most adventures are less than half an hour away from each favored campground, and I've tried to highlight activities that won't require you to get back into your car, even for the entire weekend if you so prefer. Each chapter serves as a comprehensive guide for a weekend of outdoor activities, with lodging and restaurant recommendations, activity descriptions, outfitters, contact information, directions, and plenty of tips.

In reality, there's more adventure in each chapter than most people could—or would want to—tackle in 48 hours, so you can piece together a weekend itinerary based on your skill level and favorite activities. Area maps of each destination and detailed directions will help you get the lay of the land and maximize your time outside. And, of course, nothing's stopping you from making multiple trips to your favorite destinations! Also, don't feel obligated to stick exclusively to the book's suggestions if you encounter other activities that strike your fancy; I've always planned my trips but have no problem changing them up as I go along.

LODGING ⛺

In each chapter, I recommend a "top pick" campground, most of them in state parks, based on aesthetics, amenities, cleanliness, privacy, spaciousness, seasonal dates, and, most important, proximity to recreational opportunities. That said, not all campgrounds—or all campsites—are equal. Some areas with terrific recreational opportunities have only an average campground nearby; other times, the campground and the amenities in the park are so good you won't need much else. While I love setting up my tent in a big site with scenic views, with thick forest to provide solitude, what I appreciate most on a time-crunched weekend trip is being close to all the fun things I want to do. In most cases, I also suggest a backup campground. Sometimes you might even prefer the backup because of its location or the type of camping it offers (walk-in versus drive-in, for example), but sometimes there can be a bit of a drop-off in quality between the first and second choices.

Everybody's preference in campsites is different. I am picky and have spent years jotting down notes when I travel through park campgrounds, using them for reference when I book sites in the future. Your preferences may be different than mine, but in each chapter I have tried to give both general and specific advice about campsites. You may well end up in a campsite on your first visit to a park that isn't as "good" as one you see across the campground. That's OK. Take notes like I did, and the next time around you can reserve that great one.

Keep in mind that state parks in Minnesota require all campsites to be reserved. Look for more information in the book on how to snag the best sites! State forest campgrounds, on the other hand, make their campsites available on a first-come, first-served basis, so you can use them for last-minute trips when state parks are full, and you can drive around the campgrounds to find the best available spot.

In case your idea of an awesome weekend doesn't involve curling up in a tent, I also cover alternate park accommodations, such as camper cabins, yurts, and, yes, even tepees—you'll also find details on those throughout the book. Minnesota state parks have done a great job accommodating people who want different kinds of park sleeping experiences. Of course, there may be times when you want—or need—to stay in lodging outside the park, so I've also included some options for hotels, inns, and the like.

HOW TO BE A GOOD (CAMP) NEIGHBOR

For many people, part of the goal of a camping trip is to find a little bit of peace and quiet. Sometimes, though, that's easier said than done—and there's nothing like a noisy neighbor in an adjacent campsite to put a damper on a weekend trip.

Most people do their best to keep the volume down while camping, but a few considerations will make for a good trip for you and the other people in the campground:

- When you camp, observe quiet hours (10 p.m.–8 a.m. in state parks). Many families have infants and children who turn in early, and because a lot of young ones (as well as older ones!) sleep lightly while camping, they can be easily awakened.

- A lot of campers have a long drive after work on Friday to get to their camping destination, so it's not unusual for people to be arriving at parks after dark. If you get to your campsite late at night, try your best to unload your gear without slamming car doors.

- Want to warble "Kumbaya" around the campfire? Go for it! Just don't have your singalong late at night.

- Minnesota state parks prohibit alcohol in part because drinking campers often turn into loud campers. But it's highly unlikely anyone will bother you if you just have a glass of wine or a beer.

HIKING 🥾

If you can walk, you can hike. However, not every hike is suitable for all adventurers. Keep in mind that a mile in the backcountry can feel like much more than a mile of walking around your neighborhood, and even a route on the Superior Hiking Trail can change from flat to crazy ups and downs within a short distance. I provide general information about each recommended trail, including distance, route-finding tips, and hike highlights. You'll also find directions to the trailhead and other pertinent information. At the same time, because I didn't have space for everything, if you're considering a particularly rugged or remote trail, it's a good idea to gather more information in advance of your weekend, from the trail operator or association, friends who may have hiked it, or via social media. The Superior Hiking Trail Association, for example, publishes a guidebook as well as trail maps, and the folks in their Two Harbors office are always happy to answer questions about the trail. There is also an active Facebook group of SHT hikers who can also provide information and opinions. For more information on the Superior Hiking Trail, see pages 12–13.

BIKING

You'll find places to explore on two wheels almost everywhere in Minnesota, which has an extensive collection of trails of all lengths, most of them paved, and many of them on former railroad beds that provide for nice and easy riding. Each chapter directs you to the best road/mountain biking in the area of focus; some areas have better trails for road biking, while others offer more opportunities for mountain biking. In most cases, you'll be able to find a trail that will be suitable, regardless of whether you're riding alone and want to test your endurance or you're taking the kids out on training wheels.

■ Biking in Crow Wing County

PADDLING

Grab that canoe, kayak, or stand-up paddleboard (SUP)! In the Land of 10,000 Lakes, there are plenty of paddling opportunities. You don't have to own a boat or have paddling experience to enjoy many of Minnesota's waterways—where possible in the book, I provide lists of outfitters who rent canoes, kayaks, SUPs, and all the gear you need. Those outfitters are also great sources of information. They can give you current conditions, suggest the best places to paddle based on your knowledge and experience, and even provide instruction.

CLIMBING

Climbing is not as popular an activity in Minnesota as it is in some places, but there are some absolutely beautiful and challenging places to climb in the state, and the number of climbers is growing. I chose a couple of locations because of the availability of climbing activities. We may not have a Yosemite in Minnesota, but we do have a Tettegouche!

If you're interested in learning more about climbing in Minnesota, check out the nonprofit Minnesota Climbers Association at mnclimbers.org.

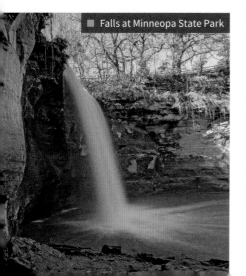

■ Falls at Minneopa State Park

OTHER ADVENTURES

You never know what fun you might find outdoors in various areas of the state that falls outside the realm of biking, hiking, and the like. Not every activity has to involve the burning of massive amounts of calories, right?! There are waterfalls to view, northern lights to photograph, and bison and trumpeter swans to watch. When appropriate in chapters of the book, I've included these kinds of activities to complement your other adventure weekend enterprises.

The Minnesota Music Hall of Fame is a popular New Ulm attraction.

RAINY DAY

With the right gear—a waterproof jacket and rain pants, a sturdy tarp, a roomy tent, and lots of towels—adventures don't have to stop in the rain. However, a rainy day can sometimes be a chance to visit places you might skip over on a sunny afternoon. I tried to include in each chapter a few places that you might enjoy when you can't get to a hiking or biking trail, and I've highlighted those that might keep the kids occupied for a few hours (instead of going crazy stuck in a tent).

FOOD AND DRINK

Campsite cooking is its own adventure, but it's also fun to check out the local food and drink scene, especially when you wake up to raindrops. Whenever possible, I suggest restaurants and breweries that are local favorites, don't require you to shower beforehand, and offer a unique and affordable experience. I've always found one of the pleasures of traveling around Minnesota on camping expeditions to be running across a little café favored by the locals that produces a stack of pancakes or a slice of cherry pie that can make the whole weekend worthwhile. And with the growing popularity of craft beer, you'll also find references to outstanding local brew. I'm sure I left out some fine places, so certainly feel free to look around the towns near where you're staying for places I haven't listed—you never know when you might find a gem.

GEAR AND RESUPPLY

Don't worry: everyone forgets something on a weekend adventure! (I won't tell you about the time I left the tent poles at home.) For items you can't live without, I've provided the locations of the closest outfitters—or the closest substitute to an outfitter—to the top campground. Of course, your ability to resupply will vary by destination. If you forget your tent, you'll be in much better shape if you're camping near a city center than a remote wilderness, so it's always wise to double-check that list before you leave home. State parks do offer gear and supplies to varying degrees—some have large shops in the visitor center, but others have only minimal supplies.

Bridge at Jay Cooke State Park

THE LEAVE NO TRACE SEVEN PRINCIPLES

The Leave No Trace Seven Principles are the bedrock of the Leave No Trace program, as promoted by the educational nonprofit Leave No Trace Center for Outdoor Ethics. They provide guidance to enjoy our natural world in a sustainable way that avoids human-created impacts. The center holds educational events around the country, and if you have an opportunity to attend one of their programs, they are well worth your while.

It seems there is heightened awareness these days of these principles, but at the same time we've seen a huge increase in use of many recreational areas, much of it by people who don't seem concerned about leaving things better than they find them. The word microtrash has even been coined to describe all the little bits of paper found on trails and in campgrounds. We all need to do a better job of following these principles.

- **Plan Ahead and Prepare** This involves knowing the regulations and special concerns for the area you'll visit, preparing for extreme weather, hazards, and emergencies. If possible, schedule your trip to avoid times of high use; you'll have more fun when it's not crowded anyway. Visit in small groups when possible and consider splitting larger groups into smaller ones.

- **Travel and Camp on Durable Surfaces** Durable surfaces include established trails and campsites, rock, gravel, dry grasses, and snow. Don't take shortcuts between trails or campsites, even those that others may have created.

  If a trail is muddy, just walk through the mud (your boots are going to get muddy eventually anyway) instead of around to the side, which widens trails and kills plant life. Don't alter established campsites and don't create your own in areas where dispersed camping is not allowed (and especially in areas where trails may travel through private land).

■ Winter camp at Tettegouche State Park

- **Dispose of Waste Properly** You've heard it before, but it's worth repeating: Pack it in; pack it out. Inspect your campsite and rest areas for trash or spilled foods, and pack out all trash, leftover food, and litter. Deposit solid human waste in catholes dug 6–8 inches deep and at least 200 feet from water, camp, and trails. Cover and disguise the cathole when finished. OK, I know it's not fun, but pack out toilet paper and hygiene products—it's not so bad if you prepare for the chore by bringing appropriate bags. To wash yourself or your dishes, carry water 200 feet away from streams or lakes and use small amounts of biodegradable soap. Scatter strained dishwater.

- **Leave What You Find** Sure, it is tempting to bring home a souvenir from your trip—a rock or flower or shell. (Take only pictures; leave only footprints.) It's just one, right? No, it's one times everybody else who does the same. So don't. Preserve the past: examine, but do not touch, cultural or historic structures and artifacts. Leave rocks, plants, and other natural objects as you find them. Avoid introducing or transporting non-native species. Do not build structures or furniture or dig trenches. Check your campsite carefully when you leave to make sure you have not left a tent stake or clothesline behind.

- **Minimize Campfire Impacts** Campfires can cause lasting impacts to the environment, so limit the number of fires you have and keep them small. Use a lightweight stove for cooking and enjoy a candle lantern for light. Where fires are permitted, use established fire rings, fire pans, or mound fires. Use only sticks from the ground that can be broken by hand, and do not take branches from live trees. Pay attention to the rules of a particular park about gathering firewood. Burn all wood and coals to ash, put out campfires completely, then scatter cool ashes; check, double-check, and triple-check your fire is out before you leave your campsite. Please read the section on page 10 about firewood transportation rules in Minnesota.

- **Respect Wildlife** Observe wildlife from a distance. Do not follow or approach them, even if you're lugging that expensive camera and feel you just have to have a close-up. Never feed animals; feeding wildlife damages their health, alters natural behaviors, and exposes them to predators and other dangers.

Sandhill crane at Sherburne NWR

   Protect wildlife and your food by storing rations and trash securely, following rules and established principles for boxing, hanging, or otherwise keeping food away from critters. (Losing your food ruins a trip really fast anyway.) Control pets at all times, or leave them at home. Avoid wildlife during sensitive times: mating, nesting, raising young, or winter.

- **Be Considerate of Other Visitors** There's also a sidebar on page 4 about how to be a good neighbor. It really comes down to respecting other visitors and protecting the quality of their experience. On the trail, be courteous and yield to other hikers, especially when they are going up and you are going down. Take breaks, and camp away from trails and other visitors. Avoid loud voices and noises, and use your headphones if you want to listen to music.

© 1999 by the Leave No Trace Center for Outdoor Ethics: lnt.org

STAYING SAFE

It's so easy to hop out of your car and head on down a hiking trail that we sometimes forget to take precautions. Most likely you're going to complete that hike without a problem, but what if the temperature climbs and you didn't bring any water? Or you get lost and didn't bring a map? Minor issues can become big ones when you're not prepared—but the good news is that it really doesn't take much to do the simple things to keep yourself safe.

A good place to start before any trip is with the list of Ten Essentials, popularized by the Boy Scouts of America and the Mountaineers, a Seattle-based organization for outdoor adventurers. You may see variations of the list in different places, but all are essentially the same. What has changed a bit over the years is that the list now contains general categories instead of just specific items.

The list below should be used as a starting point for any outdoor adventure. Will you need every item on every trip? Hope not! But every item here could end up worth its weight in gold if you ever run into a situation where you need it. And who can predict when that might be?

- Navigation: map, compass, altimeter, GPS device, personal locator beacon (PLB), or satellite messenger
- Headlamp: plus extra batteries
- Sun protection: sunglasses, sun-protective clothes, and sunscreen
- First aid: including foot care and insect repellent (as needed)
- Knife: plus a gear repair kit
- Fire: matches, lighter, tinder, and/or stove
- Shelter: carried at all times (can be a light emergency bivy)
- Extra food: beyond the minimum expectation
- Extra water: beyond the minimum expectation
- Extra clothes: beyond the minimum expectation

SOME CONSIDERATIONS FOR ADVENTURE WEEKENDS IN MINNESOTA

CELL PHONE COVERAGE

I'm about as techie as you can get without making a living as an IT guy. But one of the reasons I go for outdoor adventures is that they give me a chance to disconnect from the electronic world, to relax and decompress. But the reality is that many families like to be able to stay in touch with the outside world during outdoor weekends, whether it's to be able to communicate in case of an emergency or simply for entertainment.

As you travel around to state parks throughout Minnesota, you'll find that some have great cell phone coverage and others don't, and you may have a good connection on one visit but not on the next. Not surprisingly, the parks that are closer to popula-tion centers tend to have better coverage. If it's important that you are able to use a cell phone during your visit, it's wise to check with the park or your carrier about coverage before making reservations.

The Minnesota Department of Natural Resources, which operates the parks, understands that the ability to use connected devices is important to many families and can help draw them to parks. As a result, they are adding Wi-Fi capabilities to some campgrounds, and I'd be surprised if it's not a standard feature when new camp-grounds are opened and others are renovated. To find out which parks have Wi-Fi, visit dnr.state.mn.us/state_parks/starter_kit/techie.html.

FIREWOOD

It's expensive to buy firewood a few sticks at a time each time you camp. So in the interest of economy, I used to purchase firewood in larger quantities, store it in my garage, and then shrink-wrap individual bundles the right size for each camping trip.

But that strategy has been halted by the emerald ash borer, an invasive forest insect that has killed millions of ash trees since it was discovered in 2009. As many as a billion more ash trees in the state's forests remain threatened, as do residential ash plantings.

In an effort to keep the pest from spreading via firewood moved around by camp-ers, a state statute was enacted in 2017 requiring campers to buy firewood from the place they camp or from a nearby approved vendor. The firewood has to be non-ash, harvested from and purchased in the same county where it will be used, or other-wise certified by the Minnesota Department of Agriculture or the USDA Animal and Plant Health Inspection Service.

The firewood you buy from a state park should have a label on the bundle show-ing it has been approved. If you buy it outside the park, make sure it has a label, and get a receipt as proof of where it was purchased.

If you try to bring unapproved firewood to your campground, you'll be asked to give it up—or go home. You can be fined for using unapproved firewood.

I no longer bring my own wood to my campsites. It costs me a few bucks more buying my firewood in small bundles now—but it's a small price to pay for helping to protect our forests.

Firewood may not be available for purchase at a state park if you arrive after the park office is closed. If you need to pick up firewood outside the park, this web-site lists locations where wood is available near campgrounds throughout the state: firewoodscout.org/s/MN.

I CAN!

If you've picked up this book, you probably have an interest in camping. Maybe you're a veteran outdoors person. But perhaps you're interested but have never camped . . . and have no clue where to start.

Trial and error is one way, but making rookie mistakes is not always fun. In fact, many novice campers struggle so much out of the gate that they sour on the experi-ence for life—and that's a shame.

That's why I thought it was so cool when the Minnesota Department of Natural Resources launched **I Can!** a few years ago. It's a series of programs designed to help people, especially families with children, try outdoor activities such as fishing, paddling, mountain biking—and camping.

The one- or two-night camping programs take place in a state park group camp, and everything you need—except for sleeping bags and food—is provided. The DNR furnishes tents, sleeping pads, cooking gear, and other basic equipment. There's instruction on setting up camp, cooking, and starting a campfire, and some of the programs also include sessions on topics including geocaching and nature photography.

Up to six people in a family can take part, for a very reasonable fee of $60 for the one-night program and $85 for the two-night version. About two dozen sessions are held each year, at parks throughout the state.

I Can! is a great way to start your camping career off on the right foot. For more information, go to dnr.state.mn.us/state_parks/ican/camp.html.

KEEP A CLEAN CAMP

I've been on about 300 camping trips in the last couple of decades, and I can count on one hand the number of times I've had wildlife come into my camp (not counting mosquitoes). Once it was a bear in the Boundary Waters Canoe Area, but in drive-in campgrounds, it has always been raccoons.

When I think back on those occasions, in most if not all of them, I failed to take simple precautions that might have prevented the animal visits. At least once, I left out part of a dinner when I went to bed. I don't do that anymore.

The simple fact is that when you visit any of the campgrounds in this book, your chances are slim that you'll be bothered by wildlife. They get even slimmer if you follow basic rules.

Animals are not coming into camp to say hello or to do you harm. They want food. You're unlikely to see an animal in camp if you don't leave food where it will attract them. The easiest way is to keep your food inside your vehicle. In parks where animal encounters are more likely, or where you might be camping away from your car, you will find lockable boxes at each site. When you're away from camp, or at night, wrap up any food tightly, put it in the box, and secure the latch. Even better, before putting the food in the box, put it in a storage bag (available at outdoors stores) that blocks smells.

How about storing food in an unlocked cooler? I wouldn't recommend it. In a park known for raccoon problems, I once put food in a cooler and stacked firewood on top, then wedged the cooler under a picnic table bench. Although they didn't get the cooler open, raccoons still showed up. Why? The most likely explanation is that they had, over time and from previous campers, come to associate coolers with an easy meal.

Also, it helps immeasurably to keep a clean camp. Don't leave empty soda cans around or crumbs on the picnic table. Stash any trash in your vehicle or take it to a receptacle out of camp.

It may seem obvious that inside your tent is the worst place to store food. But it wasn't obvious to my wife, back in her single days when she went camping with friends. A ranger warned the group that the raccoons were active and they should not leave their food out. To them, "not out" meant in the tent. It didn't work—five (yes, five) raccoons shredded the tent fly in the middle of the night, trying to get at the pound of bacon they'd brought for breakfast. You don't want to lose your tent. Or go hungry for breakfast.

STATE PARK RESERVATIONS

Until 2016, about 30% of campsites at each Minnesota state park were kept open for campers arriving at the park with no reservations—the sites were unavailable for phone or online booking. But that spring the Department of Natural Resources (DNR) changed its policy to allow every one of the 5,000 state park campsites to be reserved ahead of time.

The DNR made the switch because they'd heard too much grumbling from families who had driven hours on a Friday afternoon only to find that the nonreservable sites at their destination park had been snapped up by others arriving earlier in the day, leaving the latecomers with no place to pitch their tent. The demand for sites was simply higher than the supply.

So, if you want to visit Minnesota's most popular parks, you have to plan far ahead. The state's booking system permits reservations up to a year in advance, and it's not unusual for prime sites in prime parks over prime weekends to be gone minutes after they go on sale. Tettegouche State Park reservations have become the Taylor Swift tickets of the camping world.

If you do have difficulty finding the campsite you want for the date you want, there are options. One is to keep checking back—plans change, and cancellations do happen.

But if your ideal weekend nears and there aren't any cancellations, or you aren't the type who can or wants to plan much in advance, another option is to try a less-popular state park nearby (and maybe discover a new favorite in the process). In fact, when it made the policy change, the DNR also eliminated the usual reservation fee ($7 online or $10 by phone) for bookings made on the day of the stay, just to help encourage campers to make last-minute reservations.

In 2018, as a follow-up to changing the reservation system, the DNR revamped its reservation website to provide better electronic accessibility for people with disabilities, a mapping feature, and a snapshot of what's open on a particular date for multiple parks. The DNR also is increasing the number of campsite photos that can be viewed before making a reservation. You can access the reservation system at dnr.state.mn.us /state_parks/reservations.html.

SUPERIOR HIKING TRAIL

Minnesota is home to one of the nation's best long-distance hiking paths, the 310-mile Superior Hiking Trail (SHT). You'll see reference to the SHT in several chapters of this book. Sure, it may not get the same kind of attention as its longer brethren, such as the Appalachian Trail or the Pacific Crest Trail, but for those who hike it, it gets just as much love.

The trail extends from the Minnesota–Wisconsin border near Jay Cooke State Park up the north shore of Lake Superior to the Canadian border. It winds its way up the shore through the Sawtooth Mountains, offering both easy, flat sections and portions with elevation changes that will challenge even the fittest hiker. Views from the trail are varied and, frankly, astonishing—from ethereal forests of birch and aspen to the shimmering massive lake seen from ridgeline peaks.

What's particularly appealing about the trail to backpackers is that it features 93 campsites, all first come, first served and free of charge. Additionally, the trail offers numerous trailheads that make it easy to walk the trail for days or to go in for a quick overnighter. The trail is well maintained by hundreds of volunteers as well as trail personnel at the Superior Hiking Trail Association (SHTA), and with excellent signage and blazes, it's easy to follow. You'll find mention in chapters of this book of shuttle transportation services that allow hikers to park a car, hike the trail, and then be driven back to their vehicle.

The SHTA, a nonprofit organization, builds and maintains the trail and does a great job promoting its use. As traffic has increased on the trail in recent years (due in part to the popularity of the book and movie, *Wild*), the group has begun focusing on needs to be done today and in the future to keep the trail a treasure.

The SHT is well worth checking out, whether you do it as part of one of the chapters in this book or not. The SHTA has an excellent website at superiorhiking.org and publishes a book, the comprehensive *Guide to the Superior Hiking Trail*, now in its eighth edition. If you take advantage of the trail, I strongly encourage that you join the SHTA to provide financial support to this incredible resource.

■ One of the many spectacular vistas from the Superior Hiking Trail

Check out the hiking trails at Glendalough State Park.

BATTLE LAKE

The western border of Minnesota, which snuggles up against the Dakotas, spans more than 400 miles, but there isn't much population along that line, except for Fargo/Moorhead and Grand Forks. In other words, there's a fair chance you've never been out in that territory for any reason, let alone seeking outdoor adventure. But if that's the case, you're missing out. There's a great spot I love that is anchored by Battle Lake, a nice little town of 800 people about an hour east of the border, 80 miles due west of Brainerd and roughly a 3-hour trek from the Twin Cities. While there is a resort presence in the area, Battle Lake is an unspoiled, well-kept town, with its biggest advantage being that it's just 4 miles from Glendalough State Park—a true gem of the Minnesota state park system.

Areas included: Battle Lake, Glendalough State Park, Glendalough Trail, Central Lakes Trail

Adventures: Camping, biking, hiking, paddling, exploring

Directions: From the Twin Cities, take I-94 northwest for about 155 miles. Take Exit 77 to MN 78 N in Pelican Lake Township. Follow MN 78 about 20 miles to Battle Lake, then continue on MN 78 an additional 4 miles north to MN 16, where you will turn right into Glendalough State Park.

BATTLE LAKE

1 Battle Lake Inn and Suites
2 Central Lakes Cycle
3 Central Lakes Trail Parking Area & Access Point
4 Galloping Goose Rentals
5 Glendalough Lodge
6 Glendalough State Park
7 Glendalough State Park yurts
8 Lakes Area Community Center
9 Phelps Mill County Park
10 Prairie Wetlands Learning Center
11 Prospect House and Civil War Museum
12 The Rusty Nail
13 Smackin' Cakes
14 The Williams Company Store & Deli

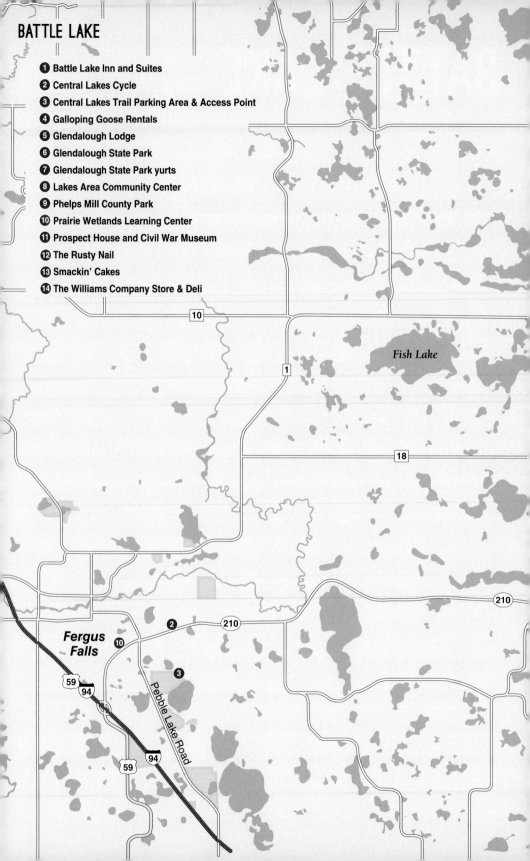

Fish Lake

Fergus Falls

Pebble Lake Road

Pickerel Lake

Otter Tail Lake

Phelps
Mill Road

9

45

1

78

Lake
Blanche

5

Annie
Battle
Lake

Glendalough
State Park

7

6

78

83

*Battle
Lake*

West Battle Lake

1

11 **13**

8

4

12

210

Clitherall
Lake

78

S. Silver
Lake Road

78

Lake
Shore
Drive

W. Silver Lake Drive

Glenhaven
Lane

1

Lake
Avenue

N. McKinley
Avenue

Dunton
Street W.

14

Summit
Street E.

Main Street W.

8 **11**

4 **13**

Holdt Street W.

12

Front
Street

Rokmar
Road

N

2 miles

2 kilometers

TOP PICK

GLENDALOUGH STATE PARK (MINNESOTA DEPARTMENT OF NATURAL RESOURCES) *24869 Whitetail Lane, Battle Lake; 218-864-0110; dnr.state.mn.us /state_parks/park.html?id=spk00167. $17–$21/night for cart-in campground, 22 sites; $13–$15/night for canoe-in sites, 3 sites; $50–$60/night for yurts, 2 yurts; $60–$70/ night for camper cabins (with electricity), 4 camper cabins; reservations required; sites have picnic table, fire ring, grill, flush and vault toilets, water, and hot showers (available March 31–early October, but check with park for specific dates); cart-in sites, yurts, and camper cabins only available Thursday–Sunday from early October to March 1. When water is not available in campgrounds, it can be found outside the park office or near the yurts. State park permit required ($35 annual, $7 daily).*

■ Cart-in camping

You won't find a single travel trailer or RV at Glendalough—there's no place for them! Glendalough, which surrounds the Annie Battle (335 acres) and Molly Stark (152 acres) Lakes, is a quiet, relaxing destination because it offers *only* a cart-in campground (although it has camper cabins too), on the west side of Annie Battle, along with three very secluded canoe-in sites on the southeast side. Additionally, Glendalough is one of only three parks in the state where you can stay in a yurt—an insulated canvas tent with a wood floor and wood-stove. The yurts are located near the canoe-in sites.

The 22 cart-in sites and the camper cabins are well spaced throughout a large, heavily wooded campground, making for plenty of privacy. The carts you use to tote your camping gear are stored right next to the parking lot, near the restrooms and shower building. The closest campsites are less than 100 yards away from parking, including sites 22 and 24, which are nearest the lake. For maximum seclusion along the lake side, try sites 15, 17, or 19. Many visitors bring along their bicycles, and if you're in a site at the far end of the campground (a little more than 400 yards) away from the restrooms, it's a fast and easy ride between on a flat, hard trail (it's a short walk as well).

WELCOME TO THE
GLENDALOUGH YURTS
ON ANNIE BATTLE LAKE
↖ 20' EAGLE   16' OSPREY ↗

OCCUPIED

A different kind of shelter

Canoe-in sites can be reached by an easy paddle across the small lake. If you don't have your own watercraft, you can rent one from the park (see information on page 22), but be aware that rentals are not available after 5 p.m.

There are a variety of ways to haul your gear to the yurts, which are a very cool place to stay if you're looking for solitude but don't want to pitch a tent. Although you can backpack into the yurt sites, the best recommendation is to leave your vehicle at the northwest corner of the park, near the rental facility (there are signs for parking), and use a provided cart. You can pull your cart along the paved bike trail, clockwise around the lake, for about 2 miles. I've also seen campers use rope to tie a cart to the back of a bicycle and pedal to their yurt, which looked like a pretty good system. Don't worry about carrying water or firewood—that's provided at the yurts. *Note:* If you have a yurt reserved, when you arrive at the park, inquire about where you can find a cart. Sometimes they are not in the parking location and may need to be moved there.

Cart storage at Glendalough

As a bit of trivia, two future U.S. presidents visited Glendalough when it was a private retreat. Dwight D. Eisenhower stopped by in 1952, just two months before he was elected president. Richard Nixon visited in 1956, when he was Eisenhower's vice president.

Directions From Battle Lake, drive 4 miles north on MN 78 to MN 16, where you will turn right into Glendalough.

CAMPER CABINS

The Minnesota Department of Natural Resources wisely realized some years back that not everyone interested in staying overnight in a state park wants to sleep in a tent, especially during the colder months of the year. Yes, a few parks have long operated lodges or group centers, but they didn't offer much in the way of an outdoors experience. So, to bridge the gap between a tent and a hotel room, the state began building camper cabins at state parks, offering park visitors a place in the woods but a roof over their heads.

The option proved extremely popular. Today, more than a third of all state parks have camper cabins, as many as six in some parks, and there are about 90 of them in total.

The wooden cabins are 12-by-16-foot structures with bunk beds, mattresses, a table, and benches. Bring sleeping bags, cooking gear, and food, and you're pretty much set. Some cabins have electric heat or woodstoves and are open year-round; those without heat are available only in warmer months. All cabin locations offer picnic tables and fire rings, and many have electricity and screened porches (the latter an addition to the more recently built cabins). Restrooms or vault toilets are located near each cabin. Some cabins, like those at Lake Maria State Park, require a hike to reach, but most offer adjacent parking.

The cabins are in demand, especially on weekends, so if you're interested in staying in one, be sure to book early. For more information visit dnr.state .mn.us/state_parks/camper_cabins.html; cabin locations are at dnr.state .mn.us/state_parks/camper_cabin_locations.html.

BACKUP BASE CAMP

Glendalough is really the only campground in the Battle Lake area that provides wilderness-style accommodations.

■ Grab an espresso in Battle Lake before your adventure.

INDOOR LODGING

Frankly, if you're looking to put a roof over your head, we'd recommend one of the Glendalough camper cabins or yurts. A number of resorts dot the area around Battle Lake and provide another lodging option; you can find more information at the website for the Lakes Area Community Center at lakesarea communitycenter.org. If you need a place to stay indoors in Battle Lake, here's where I would go:

Battle Lake Inn and Suites *102 Glen Haven Drive, Battle Lake; 218-862-2500; battlelakeinn.com; $129–$299/night*

Battle Lake Inn and Suites is located on the north edge of town, about as close to Glendalough as you're going to get. It's a nice little inn, clean and well maintained, that offers private entrances (we used to call this a motel). If a standard room is too small for your group, suites are available with kitchenettes and up to three bedrooms.

HIKING ⬤

There's nothing preventing you from hiking some or all of the 12-mile Glendalough Trail, designed primarily for biking (see below), but there are better options for hoofing it in the park.

Annie Battle Lake Trail *About 3.3 miles*

There are numerous places to pick up this trail, but the cart-in campground is a good place to start. Go south for a counterclockwise trip around the lake, which will take you on a relatively flat grassy trail past the group camp and around to the canoe-in and yurt sites. As you head north, you'll share the paved trail with bikes, but as you intersect the Lake Emma Trail, you can head back into the woods on the dirt trail.

Take some time to look at the beautiful lodge, originally part of a hunting camp, and stop at the visitor center before crossing Old Camp Bridge and heading back to the campground. The buildings were part of the original property when it was owned by the *Minneapolis Tribune* newspaper as a private retreat.

Beaver Pond Interpretive Trail *About 1.5 miles*

This loop starts in the lodge area of the park and heads northwest through the woods before doubling back along the southwest shore of Blanche Lake. Signs posted along the trail note cultural and natural history of the area.

BIKING ⬤

The 12-mile **Glendalough Trail,** which revitalized the community and doubled visitorship to the state park, is a perfect way to go from Glendalough into Battle Lake. If you want to remain in the park, the 10-foot-wide paved trail goes around Annie Battle and Molly Stark Lakes. But you can also take it all the way in to Battle Lake, or start at the trailhead in town, located at the Lakes Area Community Center (112 W. Main St.). The trail goes north out of Battle Lake, turning northeast as it hugs the western shore of West Battle Lake before veering north to the park and around the lakes. A trail map can be found at morethanatrail.com/wp-content/uploads/2017/Glendalough-Trail-Map.pdf.

If you're looking for a longer ride, and don't mind driving a bit to the trailhead, the 55-mile paved **Central Lakes Trail** runs from Fergus Falls southeast to Osakis. The trail is built on a former railroad line, and while it passes through eight small communities, the

■ Glendalough Trail

route is generally so secluded you'll feel like you're far away from any other human being. More information and a map of trailheads can be found at centrallakestrail.com.

Directions From Glendalough to Fergus Falls: Go south on MN 78 to Battle Lake and turn right on MN 210. Follow 210 about 17 miles to Fergus Falls.

■ Fishing on Annie Battle Lake

PADDLING ⊗

A lodge and trail center sit at the northwest corner of Glendalough, along Annie Battle Lake. Just before you reach the lodge, you'll spot the Galloping Goose facility, which rents canoes, kayaks, and stand-up paddleboards, as well as fishing boats with electric motors, and has concessions too. It's open daily Memorial Day–Labor Day, and on weekends otherwise during the season. As a Department of Natural Resources heritage fishery lake, all electronic devices—depth finders, GPS units, and underwater cameras—are banned here, as are gas motors.

If you decide to cast a line, you can borrow angling gear from the park office. Minnesota residents do not need a fishing license on Annie Battle or Molly Stark Lakes. Nonresidents will need to pick up a license from the DNR online or at a sporting goods store or bait shop.

There's a creek that connects Annie Battle and Molly Stark Lakes with the much larger Blanche Lake to the north, but because motorized boats are allowed on Blanche, it's not always a quiet experience.

OTHER ADVENTURES ⊕

Phelps Mill (and County Park) *29035 County Road 45, Underwood; 218-826-6159; co.otter-tail.mn.us/570/Phelps-Mill-County-Park*

It's a pretty 11-mile drive from Glendalough to Phelps Mill. The flour mill and dam were built in the late 1800s and closed in 1939. Otter Tail County has operated the location as a recreational site since 1965. You can visit the mill for a self-guided tour and spend time relaxing in the scenic park next to the Otter Tail River.

Inspiration Peak is about 20 miles southeast of Glendalough, in Otter Tail County. It's the highest point in the county at 1,750 feet, offering a scenic view of nine lakes and three counties. A wayside park is at the location, just northwest of the little town of Urbank. To get there from Glendalough, drive south on MN 78 through Battle Lake, and after about 12 miles, turn left on County Road 38. Go about 6 miles and turn left on 435th Avenue; almost immediately turn right on 120th Street. (As an aside, just south of the park is a nice little restaurant called the Peak Supper Club. It's at 43517 CR 38 in Clitherall.)

Fort Juelson is not much to look at these days compared to what it was, but it provides a pleasant little walk up a grassy hill, with a nice view, and benches to sit on and look out over the countryside. An earthen fort was constructed on the site in 1876, following rumors that American Indians were attacking homesteads and villages in the area after Custer's defeat at Little Big Horn. Many settlers fled, and work began to construct the fort. Even though the rumors proved false, the fort was completed in case future protection was needed. The remains of the barricade can be seen at the site, now owned by Otter Tail County. The fort, which is on the National Register of Historic Places, is situated on the hilltop in Tordenskjold Township, 2 miles east of Underwood. The location is marked with a flagpole that rises above the surrounding land. The fort is about 10 miles from Glendalough and 6 miles from Battle Lake. To reach it from Battle Lake, go south on MN 78 and turn right on MN 210 on the edge of town. Drive 5.8 miles, turn right on 315th Avenue, and look for the parking lot on the right.

RAINY DAY 😎

Prospect House and Civil War Museum *403 N. Lake Ave., Battle Lake; 218-864-4008; prospecthousemuseum.org*

Guided tours of this 1882 Georgian-style mansion are $8 for adults and $5 for children. The lower level of the house is a Civil War museum, recounting the service of James A. Colehour, who built the home. There is an extensive collection of Lincoln memorabilia. Call the museum for operating hours, tour times, and reservations.

Phelps Mill on the Otter Tail River

Prairie Wetlands Learning Center *602 MN 210 East, Fergus Falls; 218-998-4480; visitfergusfalls.com/prairie-wetlands-learning-center*

This beautiful facility includes 330 acres of native and restored prairie, 28 wetlands, and 3.5 miles of trails. A visitor center, open 8 a.m.–4 p.m., has a large exhibit area.

FOOD AND DRINK

There are enough lakes in this part of Minnesota to make it something of a resort area, although they're scattered around enough that, especially during the week, you'll find Battle Lake relatively quiet. There are the resort-style dining options, such as the well-known Zorbaz on the Lake (at 36108 CR 72, which is actually 6 miles north of town, on Ottertail Lake) and Battle Lake Boathouse (112 Lake Ave. S.), among others. But if you're looking for something quick during a break in your bike ride, here are a couple of places to try:

The Williams Company Store & Deli *102 W. Summit St., Battle Lake; 218-862-6906; thewilliamscompanystore.com*

If you're expecting to see a restaurant when you enter the Williams Company Store through its patio entrance on Summit, don't be surprised—the upstairs is a gift shop. Once inside, look for the stairs to the lower level, where the deli is located. You'll find an excellent selection of sandwiches for breakfast, lunch, or an early dinner (they close at 6 p.m.). If you're a coffee connoisseur, try one of the excellent espresso drinks.

Smackin' Cakes *114 Lake Ave. S., Battle Lake; 218-862-4900; smackincakes.com*

Operating May to September, Smackin' Cakes opens at 8 a.m. and has coffee and a tempting selection of scones if you're looking for something to start your morning. For a treat later in the day, you'll find cupcakes and, in a nod to the latest craze, an extensive cookie dough bar.

The Disgruntled Taproom *735 2nd Ave., Perham; 218-346-4677; disgruntledbeer.com*

Perham is a little over 20 miles north of Glendalough, but if you're a fan of great craft beer, it might be worth a visit. Disgruntled brews a wide variety of creative beers, and their taproom is a good place for sampling. Menace is their American stout, and there's an American brown ale they dub Bulletproof. Most interesting is the Contaminated Lemonade, a sour German wheat beer known as gose, which has a lemon-lime flavor.

The Rusty Nail *123 Lake Ave. S., Battle Lake; 218-864-2600; rustynailbl.com*

If you're looking for a cold one closer to the park, you can't go wrong with the Rusty Nail. They don't brew their own beer, but the selection is massive and ever-changing. The Rusty Nail is especially supportive of Minnesota brewers, so look on the menu for selections from Fulton (Minneapolis), Bent Paddle (Duluth), and Liftbridge (Stillwater). Oh, and the place serves a pretty good burger as well.

■ The lodge at Glendalough State Park features displays on the park's history.

GEAR AND RESUPPLY 🛒

Galloping Goose Rentals *112 Main St. E., Battle Lake; 218-731-7181; gallopinggooserentals.net*

Besides its location in Glendalough State Park, Galloping Goose has a place in the central part of town that offers rentals if you'd like to bike to the park and back, and it also carries some bike supplies. You can also rent watercraft for use in nearby lakes.

Central Lakes Cycle *2010 MN 210 E., Fergus Falls; 218-739-5651; centrallakescycle.com*

The Glendalough Trail has been a boon to Battle Lake, but it still lacks a full-service bike shop. For that, you'll have to go 20 miles west to Fergus Falls.

The swinging bridge at Jay Cooke is the park's main attraction.

CARLTON

If Minnesota is considered fly-over country, then some people might call Jay Cooke State Park drive-by land. If you're eager to get to the North Shore for a weekend or vacation, it's easy to speed by signs for the park on I-35 as you begin the approach to Duluth. Granted, Jay Cooke is not ignored by everyone; the park's swinging bridge is a popular attraction. But the attention the bridge gets sometimes obscures the fact that there's plenty more to Jay Cooke and the surrounding environs than just traversing the iconic span that crosses the St. Louis River. Jay Cooke is a classic Minnesota state park, a wilderness steeped in history with all the recreational opportunities you would want for a weekend adventure, no matter what your fancy. The St. Louis, for example, is the only river in Minnesota designated as a whitewater trail, and it's a must if you're interested in rafting. For your next trip "up north," don't go quite as far as everyone else does—stop short instead and head for Jay Cooke.

Areas included: Jay Cooke State Park, Fond du Lac State Forest, Carlton, Duluth, Spirit Mountain

Adventures: Camping, biking, hiking, paddling, exploring

Directions: From the Forest Lake area north of the Twin Cities, go about 100 miles north on I-35. Take Exit 235 to MN 210 E in Twin Lake Township and drive about 2 miles to Carlton.

CARLTON

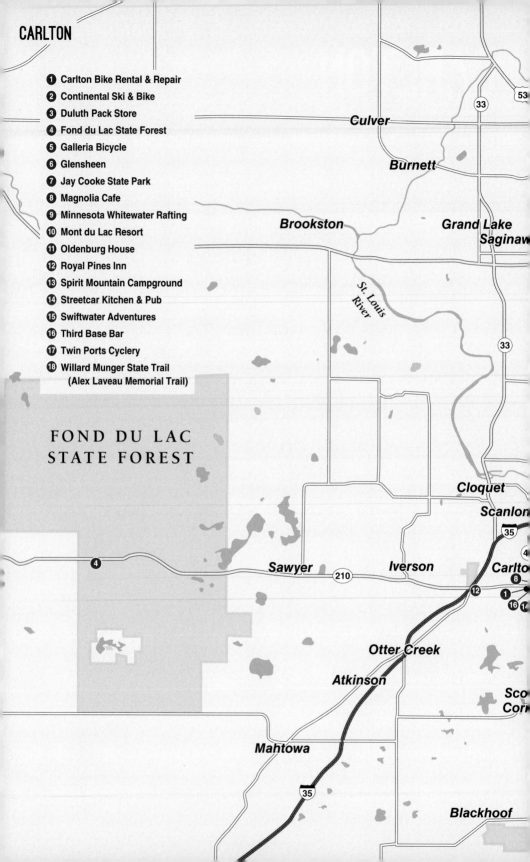

1. Carlton Bike Rental & Repair
2. Continental Ski & Bike
3. Duluth Pack Store
4. Fond du Lac State Forest
5. Galleria Bicycle
6. Glensheen
7. Jay Cooke State Park
8. Magnolia Cafe
9. Minnesota Whitewater Rafting
10. Mont du Lac Resort
11. Oldenburg House
12. Royal Pines Inn
13. Spirit Mountain Campground
14. Streetcar Kitchen & Pub
15. Swiftwater Adventures
16. Third Base Bar
17. Twin Ports Cyclery
18. Willard Munger State Trail
    (Alex Laveau Memorial Trail)

FOND DU LAC
STATE FOREST

Culver

Burnett

Brookston

Grand Lake
Saginaw

St. Louis River

Cloquet

Scanlon

Sawyer

Iverson

Carlto

Otter Creek

Atkinson

Sco
Corr

Mahtowa

Blackhoof

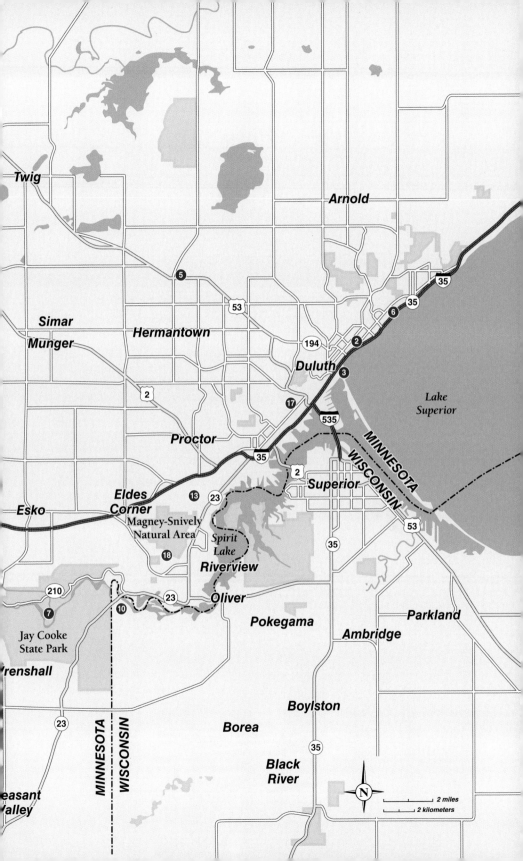

LODGING

TOP PICK

JAY COOKE STATE PARK (MINNESOTA DEPARTMENT OF NATURAL RESOURCES)
*780 MN 210, Carlton; 218-673-7000; dnr.state.mn.us/state_parks/park.html?id
=spk00187. $17–$23/night ($8 more for sites with electric hookups) for drive-in and
walk-in camping, 83 sites, 21 with electric hookups, 4 walk-in; $13–$15/night for
backpack sites, 4 sites; $60–$70/night for camper cabins, 5 cabins, electricity and
heat in all cabins; 12 sites, including 5 with electric hookups, are available for winter
camping; reservations required; sites have picnic table, fire ring, grill, showers, flush
and vault toilets; state park permit required ($35 annual, $7 daily).*

Ten inches of rain walloped northeast Minnesota in June of 2012, swelling the St.
Louis River, which then took down the famous swinging bridge in Jay Cooke State
Park. But 16 months and more than a million dollars later, the 1,200-foot-long suspension bridge was back and better than ever—restored to look like it did in 1934,
when the Civilian Conservation Corps (CCC) built it with wood and stone pillars.

The bridge is located south of MN 210 as the highway passes through the park,
with the park's campground on the northern side of the road. As you enter the
bridge parking lot, you'll see the park office, picnic areas, an amphitheater, and the
stunning River Inn Interpretive Center, a 1941 CCC project built from an igneous
rock called gabbro.

The bridge may be the focal point, but the park and nearby areas feature a wealth
of recreational opportunities, including plenty of hiking, biking, and paddling.

■ Secluded campsite at Jay Cooke State Park

In addition, the park property is dotted with beautiful buildings constructed by the CCC, all worth a visit, including the picnic shelter and bathroom building at Oldenburg Point, which is east on MN 210 from the campground, on the south side of the road. The area offers short walks to overlooks with incredible views of the river.

■ Ready for a campfire

In the winter, the park maintains 20 miles of groomed trail for cross-country skiing and sometimes adds another 12 miles if snow conditions are good. The ski trails are generally easy close to the park office but get more difficult the farther out you travel.

The campground area at Jay Cooke consists of five loops, and they differ somewhat in the relative privacy of sites. Tent campers would do well to avoid the loop to the right as you enter the campground, which has electric sites with numbers in the 40s. The best loop is at the far northeast of the campground, sites 65–80. The sites on the east side of that loop are best, with site 70 a favorite. There are also good sites on the northwest loop, numbering 4–22. I like 19, 21, and 23 in that loop.

I don't normally give away the locations of my absolute favorite campsites, but if you promise not to tell anyone else, I'll let you in on the secret at Jay Cooke. It's site 68, which is on that northeast loop. The site is officially listed as a walk-in, which means it often goes unreserved, given most people want to be snuggled up next to their vehicle. Here's the deal, though: it's only about 50 steps to the campsite from your car, which will never be out of your sight. In exchange for a little bitty tiny walk, you get the roomiest campsite I've seen in the park, a spot of heaven completely surrounded by trees. But remember—it's our little secret.

If you're interested in backpacking into a campsite, the closest to parking is a pretty little spot called High Landing, a walk of a little more than 2 miles down the Silver Creek Trail, which is also the Hiking Club trail. (For information on Hiking Club trails, see page 101.)

Directions From Carlton, take MN 210 E about 3 miles to the park.

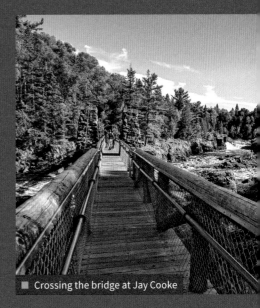
■ Crossing the bridge at Jay Cooke

■ The St. Louis River is a must for whitewater rafting.

BACKUP BASE CAMP

There are not a lot of camping options for tent campers in the immediate area around Jay Cooke, one reason why some backpackers thru-hiking the Superior Hiking Trail from south to north choose to skip the portion of the trail between Jay Cooke and Duluth. But here's one choice:

Spirit Mountain Campground
9500 Spirit Mountain Place, Duluth; 800-642-6377; spiritmt.com/campground. $39–$44/night for sites with electric hook-ups, 73 sites; $29/night for tent-only walk-in sites, 10 sites; reservations available but not required, two-night minimum on weekends; sites have picnic table, fire ring, flush toilets, and showers; some sites have cooking grates.

This campground attracts people who are heading to the nearby Spirit Mountain Adventure Park or to the lift-accessed downhill mountain biking trails (used for skiing and snowboarding in winter). The sites with hookups are generally used by recreational vehicles, but there are tent-only sites that require a short walk-in in exchange for a tiny bit of distance from the main camping area. Expect crowds during the weekends, when the mountain bike trails are open, but the place is pretty quiet on weekdays.

The address above is for the main Spirit Mountain facility. The address of the campground is 9535 W. Skyline Parkway, Duluth.

> ***Directions to the campground*** Instead of taking the MN 210 exit when you're heading north on I-35, stay on the interstate and follow it 13.9 miles to West Skyline Parkway in Proctor. Take Exit 249 and follow the parkway 1.1 miles to the campground.

INDOOR LODGING

Oldenburg House *604 Chestnut Ave., Carlton; 218-384-4835; oldenburghouse.com; $135/night*

There are only two options for overnight stays here, but they are both suites, and one even has a washer and dryer, either for a longer stay or if your outdoor adventure gets you particularly dirty! The coolest thing about this place is that it has a performance space called the Carlton Room, with dining and concerts one weekend a month (reservations required). Also, canoes and kayaks are available for use by guests.

Royal Pines Inn *1508 County Road 61, Carlton; 218-384-2071; royalpinesinn.com*

This is probably as far in style from the Oldenburg as you can get. But if you're looking for no-frills and little expense, yet something clean and well kept, it's an alternative to the chain hotels on the edge of Duluth or the pricey inns at Canal Park, Duluth's tourist hub. Hotels can be expensive in Duluth in both winter and summer! Call for rates and reservations.

HIKING

Jay Cooke has some of the better hiking of Minnesota's state parks, and plenty of it. More than 50 miles of trails crisscross the park, a few on the campground side of MN 210, but most on the other side of the bridge. The park is also home to the second-to-last southern section of the Superior Hiking Trail, which runs through Duluth all the way to the Canadian border. The longest hikes would be to the end of the SHT, southeast from the bridge, or all the way to the northeast edge of the park, at the river, via the Spruce and High Trails. Honestly, there are so many options you're best off studying the map and picking out something—one nice thing about Jay Cooke is that the trails are easy to follow. But if you insist on a couple of suggestions, here you go:

Hiking Club Trail *3.5 miles*

This nice trail will also reward you if you are in the state parks Hiking Club. (For information on the Hiking Club, see page 101.) The trail begins across the bridge. The loop follows the Silver Creek Trail, which you can take east parallel to the river before heading south away from the water. You'll begin heading back northwest at about the halfway point. When you reach the trail shelter, you'll go west and then north back to the bridge. There is a bit of a climb at the beginning, and a few hills along the route.

Superior Hiking Trail *5.9 miles*

Taking this trail from the visitor center will lead you southeast to a trailhead at Wild Valley Road, off MN 23; the trail from there leads to the southern terminus of the SHT. This rugged and occasionally steep trail shares Jay Cooke trails, including Bear Chase, Lost Lake, and Silver Creek, before it becomes solely the SHT.

Trailside view of Jay Cooke's swinging bridge

BIKING ⊘

Willard Munger State Trail

This is one of Minnesota's nicest bike trails, the highlight of which is a scenic 70-mile path that runs through three counties, beginning at Hinckley on the south end and running northwest to Duluth. On its way, the trail passes near three Minnesota state parks—Banning, Moose Lake, and finally Jay Cooke. (Besides the Hinckley–Duluth Trail, the Willard Munger State Trail includes the 16-mile Alex Laveau Memorial Trail between Wrenshall and Carlton, which requires some road riding, and the 80-mile Matthew Lourey State Trail, which has a mostly natural surface.)

■ St. Louis River from near Oldenburg Point

If you're staying at Jay Cooke, you can ride the trail without ever needing to hop in your car. A spur trail to the Munger can be accessed to the west of the entrance to the campground from MN 210. The trail, roughly a mile long, goes west from the park, then north to join the main trail east of Thomson. There is also a trailhead in Carlton, just south of the intersection of North Avenue and 3rd Street. It's about a 15-mile ride between Carlton and Duluth. The northern terminus of the trail is at a parking lot near the intersection of Grand Avenue (MN 23) and 75th Avenue West in Duluth, behind the aptly named Willard Munger Inn. (In case you were wondering, Willard Munger was a longtime Minnesota legislator who pushed hard for the creation of these trails. Bless him.) If you don't want to ride all the way to the end in Duluth, there is also a trailhead at Becks Road and 123rd Avenue West, south of Short Line Park. A map and additional information about the trail can be found at dnr.state.mn.us/state_trails /willard_munger.

Jay Cooke also provides about 5 miles of fat bike trails for winter riders. A map can be found here: files.dnr.state.mn.us/maps/state_parks/spk00187_winter_biking.pdf.

PADDLING ⊗

Many visitors to the area who want to experience whitewater rafting utilize the services of one of these local companies:

Swiftwater Adventures *121 Vermillion St., Carlton; 218-451-3218; swiftwatermn.com*

Swiftwater caters to those folks visiting the area who may want something more than a leisurely bike ride. Its whitewater rafting trips hit the wildest parts of the St. Louis River, with trips running about 2 hours and offered several times a day. They depart from 3212 Rivergate Ave. in Cloquet, which is about 9 miles from the park.

Minnesota Whitewater Rafting *3212 Rivergate Ave., Cloquet; 218-522-4446; minnesotawhitewater.com*

The company has its offices in Duluth but runs its St. Louis River rafting trips from Cloquet. Besides daily whitewater rafting trips (two daily on weekends), they offer float trip rafts you can rent for your own excursions.

OTHER ADVENTURES ⊕

Fond du Lac State Forest (Minnesota Department of Natural Resources)
Carlton County; 218-460-7020; state.mn.us/state_forests/forest.html?id=sft00018

A cautionary tale, if you'll permit me. You may, as I did on my travels researching this book, consult a map when you are near a state park to see if there are additional wilderness areas nearby. That's how, while at Jay Cooke, I found the 64,000-acre Fond du Lac State Forest, about 20 minutes west of the park. I also found how easy it is to miss details when you are pulling up a map on a smartphone. After spending the good part of an afternoon trying to find the spots marked for parking near the trails on the map, and being unable to find any road that actually reached them, I looked at the map more closely. The trails I was seeing? Only for winter use, either by hunters on foot, skiers, or snowmobilers (hence the parking). No wonder I couldn't get there! And my auto GPS was no friend, either, failing to know that the roads it was showing me were often actually minimum maintenance roads, either not drivable or abandoned and taken over by the woods. I had an interesting if frustrating drive through a beautiful state forest, but unless you want to try out for a Jeep commercial, you're probably better off looking elsewhere for recreation outside of Jay Cooke. You can, though, if you'd like, take a look at the map at files.dnr.state.mn.us/maps/state_forests/sft00018.pdf or find more information about the state forest at dnr.state.mn.us/state_forests/forest.html?id=sft00018.

Mont du Lac Resort *3125 Mont du Lac Drive, Superior, WI; 218-626-3797; mdlresort.com*

Across the big bridge into Wisconsin, this resort offers skiing, snowboarding, and tubing in winter, and disc golf, mountain biking, and archery in the summer months.

RAINY DAY 😀

If foul weather forces you into your car and in search of something to do, you're likely to end up in Duluth. You can join the other tourists down in **Canal Park** (canalpark.com), or check out the visitor's guide at visitduluth.com for other ideas. There's plenty to do, from visiting **Bob Dylan's boyhood home** (roadsideamerica.com /tip/24049) to viewing the impressive collection at the **Lake Superior Railroad Museum** (lsrm.org). If you're interested in learning more about Duluth's role as a major shipping port, it's always fun for adults and kids alike to tour the **William A. Irvin** (decc .org/william-a-irvin). And no trip to Duluth is complete without seeing the **Aerial Lift Bridge** (dot.state.mn.us/historicbridges/L6116.html). Finally, if you're hungry after a day of sightseeing, consider dining at **Grandma's Saloon & Grill** (grandmasrestau rants.com), serving up local favorites since 1976 at the foot of the Aerial Lift Bridge.

Glensheen *3300 London Road, Duluth; 218-726-8910; glensheen.org; $7–15/person for self-guided tour; other tours available*

This 39-room, 20,000-square-foot mansion, which sits on 12 acres on the shore of Lake Superior as you enter Duluth, is the most popular home tour in the state, and for good reason. For one thing, there's a real-life murder mystery associated with the house (although the tours tend to downplay it). Even without that, it's hard not to be mesmerized by the architecture, the art collection, and the ornate interior design. The craftsmanship—even in the bathrooms—is astounding. The home was built in the early 1900s, and the estate has been operated by the University of Minnesota since 1968.

FOOD AND DRINK 🚗

Dozens of dining and drinking options are in nearby Duluth, but for this chapter we're keeping you out of the city so you can sample some of the local fare closest to Jay Cooke.

Magnolia Cafe *206 3rd St., Carlton; 218-499-5911; magnoliacafecarlton.com*

Some of us (like me, maybe) can get a little cranky without our morning espresso. The Magnolia takes care of my caffeine craving, and I can get a scone or muffin to boot. Later in the day, it's good for hand-dipped ice cream or a sandwich. Try the cranberry–wild rice bread. They also have gluten-free options.

Streetcar Kitchen & Pub *232 Chestnut Ave., Carlton; 218-384-3333; streetcarkitchenandpub.com*

The Streetcar is a descendant of a restaurant that started in an actual streetcar in 1928 as the Streetcar Inn and eventually became Charlotte's Café before it closed. This is the revival—a nice local joint that specializes in burgers, flatbreads, and wraps and has a nice selection of craft beers on tap.

Third Base Bar *225 Chestnut Ave., Carlton; 218-384-4515; thirdbasebar.com*

Come for pizza, burgers, and panini, as well as live music most weekends.

■ River Inn Interpretive Center at Jay Cooke State Park

GEAR AND RESUPPLY 🛒

Carlton Bike Rental & Repair *100 Chestnut Ave., Carlton; 218-384-4696; carltonbikerental.com*

This operation is conveniently located right on the Willard Munger Trail. Besides offering repair services, they rent bikes, tandems, and child trailers.

Twin Ports Cyclery *2914 W. 3rd St., Duluth; 218-624-4008; twinportscyclery.com*

If you need to venture into Duluth, Twin Ports, which has been in business for 40 years, is a good spot for a quick repair or adjustment, or even a new bike.

Continental Ski & Bike *1305 E. 1st St., Duluth; 218-728-4466; continentalski.com*

Continental is a favorite of visitors who want to rent a bike for a spin on the Munger or to mountain bike at Spirit Mountain (they have a rental facility at the Grand Avenue Chalet). They offer sales and service and partner with The Duluth Experience to offer bike tours.

Galleria Bicycle *5225 Miller Trunk Highway, Hermantown; 218-729-9704; galleriabicycle.com*

Hermantown is about a 20-minute drive from Jay Cooke, but the folks at Galleria, open since 1959, have a talent with the wrench and were early proponents of the fat tire revolution. They're also very active in the local bike community and supporters of local trail groups.

Duluth Pack *365 Canal Park Drive, Duluth; 800-777-4439; duluthpack.com*

The maker of iconic canoe packs and other outdoor gear, luggage, and apparel has its retail operation in the Canal Park area of Duluth. It's not only a good place to pick up camping gear, but also just fun to wander through. The company, which was founded in the late 1800s, continues to make all of it packs in the Duluth area.

Biking at Cuyuna Country State Recreation Area

CROW WING COUNTY

In my highly unscientific opinion, more outdoor recreation probably goes on in Crow Wing County than in any other place in Minnesota. If you include Mille Lacs Lake, the state's second-largest body of water that sits mostly outside Crow Wing's southeastern edge, it's probably not even close. However, Crow Wing has long been favored more for resort-style recreation (think boating and fishing) than for the kind of outdoor adventures we're focusing on—and that has only increased in the past few years as the local lodges have dialed up their amenities, offering everything from first-class golf courses to sumptuous spas. But if you're more interested in muscle-powered recreation (casting for walleye doesn't count), help has arrived, courtesy mostly of the Cuyuna Country State Recreation Area.

Since its establishment in 2011, this 2,773-acre former mining site northeast of Brainerd, off the route to the resorts, has become a cycling mecca, due partly to scenic road biking paths but mostly to world-class mountain biking trails. What that means is that you can head this direction for a weekend without packing the clubs or the rods, and still find plenty to do in the outdoors (there's paddling too).

Areas included: Crow Wing State Park, Cuyuna Country State Recreation Area, Paul Bunyan State Trail, Crow Wing River, Mississippi River, Brainerd, Baxter, Ironton, Crosby

Adventures: Camping, biking, paddling, hiking, exploring

Directions: From the Twin Cities, take I-94 northwest toward Rogers, where it is about 95 miles to Crow Wing State Park. Follow I-94 about 14 miles to Exit 193 in Monticello. Exit and take Park Boulevard SE, which turns into 165th Avenue SE, about 5 miles to US 10 in Becker Township. Turn left on US 10 and continue about 55 miles, then keep right to continue on MN 371. Go about 20 miles and turn left on 60th Avenue SW/N. Koering Road, and the park will be on your left.

CROW WING COUNTY

1. The Barn
2. Croft Mine Historical Park
3. Crow Wing State Park
4. Cuyuna Country State Recreation Area
5. Cuyuna Mountain Bike Trail System
6. Cycle Path & Paddle
7. Gull Lake Recreation Area
8. Hallett House Bed & Breakfast
9. Life Cycle
10. Louie's Bucket of Bones
11. Mixed Company– A Kava House
12. North Country Cafe
13. Paul Bunyan Land
14. Pennington Mine Lake
15. Pirate's Cove Adventure Golf and Billy Bones Raceway
16. Portsmouth Campground
17. Portsmouth Mine Pit Lake
18. Red Raven Bike Café
19. Roundhouse Brewery
20. Yawkey Mine Lake yurts

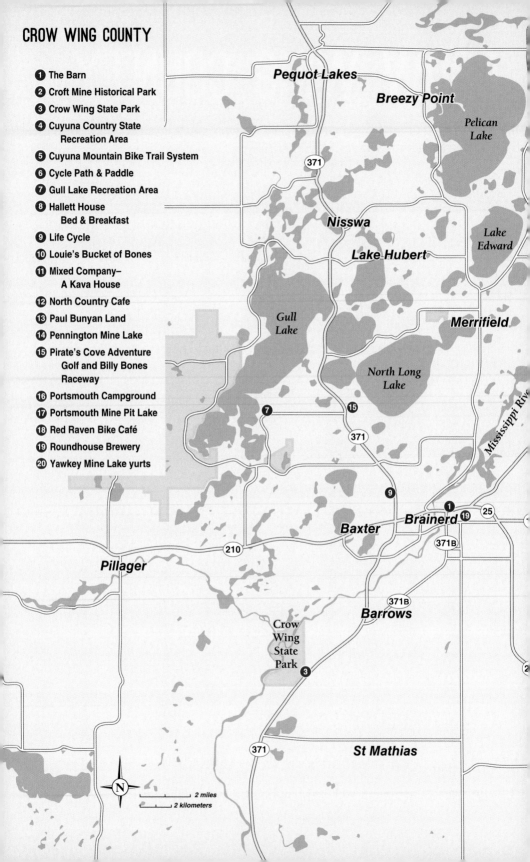

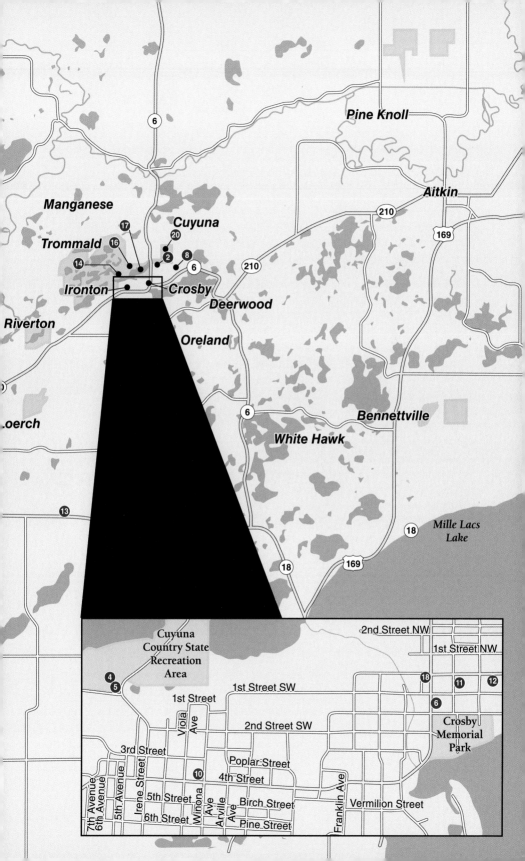

TOP PICK

CROW WING STATE PARK (MINNESOTA DEPARTMENT OF NATURAL RESOURCES) *3124 State Park Road, Brainerd; 218-825-3075; dnr.state.mn.us/state _parks/park.html?id=spk00139. $17–$21/night for drive-in sites, 59 sites, including 12 with electric hookups; $55–$65/night for camper cabin, 1 cabin, open April 1–October, no electricity or woodstove, reservations required; sites have picnic table, fire ring, grill, showers, flush and vault toilets; state park permit required ($35 annual, $7 daily).*

Crow Wing State Park is about a 2-hour drive from the Twin Cities, but it's on the prime resort-and-cabin route, so if you're coming from Minneapolis or Saint Paul, trips on a Friday afternoon will likely take longer than advertised. (Be patient, though. You'll get there.) Crow Wing State Park sits about 9 miles southwest of Brainerd. Swing into the Brainerd Lakes Welcome Center just before you enter the park to pick up maps and any informational literature you might want for the weekend. At the park you are going be to about 20 miles southwest of Cuyuna, but the 120-mile Paul Bunyan bike trail starts right here; this is also where the Crow Wing River empties into the Mississippi River, so there are paddling opportunities as well.

■ Cuyuna Country trail

Crow Wing is a typical Minnesota state park campground, albeit with a lot of campsites that are a bit smaller than average. I'd try to stay away from the dozen or so electric sites you'll see on your left when you enter the park. Sites 18–20 on the outside of the loop just past the shower building are not bad choices. Sites 21 and 32 have a little more privacy than most but are not particularly roomy. Site 38 is a good choice. In the southwest part of the campground is a short road extension with seven sites (40–46) that will get you a bit off the main drag.

BACKUP BASE CAMPS

Gull Lake Recreation Area (U.S. Army Corps of Engineers) *10867 E. Gull Lake Drive, Brainerd; 651-290-5772; recreation.gov/camping/campgrounds/233648. $26/night for drive-in sites, 39 sites, all with electric hookups; open May 1–October 15; reservations recommended, especially for weekends; sites have picnic table, fire ring, grill, flush and vault toilets, showers.*

You may notice in this book that I tend not to recommend campgrounds that cater primarily to recreational vehicles. That reflects a personal bias, and my wife sometimes chides me for being a bit of a camping snob. Guilty as charged; I do prefer sharing my outdoor space with fellow tent campers (even if we seem to be a shrinking breed) and not huge RVs. But I try my best to realize that not everyone is as picky as I am, so you can make your own choice here. Gull Lake Recreation Area offers electric hookups at all its sites, so it will have plenty of camping vehicles, but at the same time the big rigs mostly stay away because it can be difficult for them to maneuver in this park. You'll generally see a mix of pop-up campers and smaller vehicles, but yes, there are tent campers. Unlike many RV-oriented facilities, this one offers mostly roomy sites that are generally wooded, shielding you from your neighbors for a measure of seclusion. It's not the middle of the deep dark woods, certainly, but it's not bad, and if you're camping with kids, they'll enjoy the playground, the beach, and some short interpretive hiking trails.

Camping in this park is along a large loop, and the sites on the outside of the loop tend to be the best. None are located right on the water, but sites 25, 27, 28, 30, and 39 are closest.

If you've ever taken a trip to the Boundary Waters Canoe Area, you've used the same reservation system used by Gull Lake Recreation Area. Nightly camping fees are a little higher than at Minnesota state parks, but there is no reservation fee (although a service charge will be levied for changing or canceling a reservation). Campsite reservations can be made up to six months in advance.

> **Directions from Crow Wing State Park** Gull Lake Recreation Area is about 16 miles from Crow Wing State Park. Turn left out of the park onto MN 371. Go about 12 miles and turn left on Gull Lake Dam Road. The park is on your left in about 3 miles.

Cuyuna Country State Recreation Area *307 3rd Street, Ironton; 218-546-5926; dnr.state.mn.us/state_parks/park.html?id=sra00302. $15/night for drive-in and walk-in sites at the Portsmouth Campground, 33 sites, including 18 with electric hookups and 4 walk-in sites; $55/night weekdays and $65/night weekends for seven-person yurts, located along Yawkey Mine Lake with vault toilets nearby, 3 yurts available; reservations required; sites have picnic table, fire ring, grill, showers, and flush toilets in main campground; state park permit required ($35 annual, $7 daily).*

Abandoned by mining companies more than 35 years ago, this state recreation area contains six natural lakes, as well as another 15 deep lakes that were former mine pits. It's simply a beautiful location, with plenty of things to do, but it can be a challenge trying to figure out how to get from Point A to Point B, especially because you can go some distance between recreational opportunities. Get a map!

If you follow your GPS to the official park address, you'll wind up at the park office in the middle of Ironton. The office is good for information and maps. If instead you're heading straight to the campground and you're entering Ironton from the west on MN 210, you'll want to turn right on Irene Avenue and veer left on County Road 30. Stay on CR 30 as it veers right and follow it north after it crosses Serpent Creek. Follow the signs to the campground, which will be on your right.

■ Tired of busy trails? You'll find peace at Cuyuna Country SRA.

The campground is on the northwest shore of **Portsmouth Mine Pit Lake.** Only a few of the sites are shaded for privacy, although there is a fair amount of distance between them. The best sites are on the southern edge, 1–6, with 5 and 6 being the most private. Sites 10–13 are good too.

The three (seven-person) yurts—insulated structured canvas tents with wood floors—can be reserved for camping, but they are located about 4 miles away (a 10-minute drive), on the southwest side of **Yawkey Mine Lake,** and getting there from the lake's parking lot requires a short walk with your gear. Cuyuna is one of three locations in the Minnesota state camping system that has yurts, and they're a fun alternative to a tent. Firewood is provided for the indoor woodstoves during the winter months, but they have no electricity. The Binghamite and Manganese yurts have partial shade, and the Silkstone yurt is closest to water and vault toilets.

> ***Directions to Yawkey Mine Lake yurts*** From the park office, it's about 3 miles. Go east one block on 3rd Street and turn right on Curtis Street. In one block turn left on 4th Street, which turns into Oak Street and then into 3rd Avenue SW (CR 6) as it turns northeast by Serpent Lake. Follow the road until it crosses the bike trail; you'll see the trailhead on your left. Turn right, and go a little over a mile to the parking lot. Follow the directions to the yurts.

INDOOR LODGING

The resorts in the area don't exactly cater to a quick and inexpensive overnight stay, the kind you might be looking for if bad weather chases you out of a campground. There are plenty of chain hotels in the Brainerd/Baxter area to choose from. Lists of both can be found at business.explorebrainerdlakes.com/list/category/lodging. If you find yourself closer to Cuyuna, there's a Country Inn in Deerwood, as well as the Deerwood Motel, but if you're looking for something a little more interesting, here's an option:

Hallett House Bed & Breakfast *22418 MN 6, Deerwood; 218-772-0304; halletthouse.lodgify.com; $100–$150/night, five rooms, all with private baths*

Almost 100 years old, this Art Deco–style home sits on a wooded 11-acre lot, with waterfalls and pools, smack in the middle of the area's recreation. The Czech owners have done an incredible job maintaining the period charm of the home, inside and out, and they serve up a Czech breakfast that is more than just kolaches.

BIKING @

ROAD BIKING

Cuyuna Lakes State Trail is 8 miles of scenic, easy paved trail within the Cuyuna Country State Recreation Area going east from Riverton to Crosby. (Trailheads at both ends have kiosks with detailed route information.) The western trailhead is right off CR 128 on the east side of Riverton; if heading north, turn left on Rowe Road and enter the parking lot to the right. The trail travels northwest along CR 128 until it passes the north side of Blackhoof Lake, parallel to Portsmouth Mine Road. The trail then turns east toward Ironton, where a spur just past the lake goes into town. The trail crosses Serpent Creek and travels along the south side of Portsmouth Mine Pit Lake. It then crosses MN 6, where there is a trailhead and parking. You can continue on as the trail goes between the Croft Mine Historical Park and the city of Crosby. It runs along 8th Street NE, passing the Hallett Community Center before turning hard south just past 6th Avenue NE. The trail then turns east just past the Cuyuna Range Elementary School and ends at Cuyuna Road, although there is no parking there. The best map of the trail can be found online at traillink.com/trail/cuyuna-lakes-state-trail, but you'll need a (free) account to access it.

If you're staying at Crow Wing State Park, you can access the paved 120-mile **Paul Bunyan State Trail**—the longest of Minnesota's state trails—right in the park. The trail is built on a former railroad grade, so it's mostly level. Heading all the way up to the northern end near Bemidji might be a bit ambitious for the weekend, but there are several towns along the southern part of this rail-trail that make for good turnaround points, including Merrifield and Nisswa. It's 13 miles from the park to Baxter, 24 to Merrifield, and about 29 to Nisswa. Nisswa is an especially nice stop, with plenty of shops right off the trail.

Besides biking, the trail is used for hiking and in-line skating, and snowmobiling in the winter. If you're into geocaching, there are plenty of geocaches near the Paul Bunyan State Trail. If you want to learn more or participate in geocaching, visit

■ Bikers big and small love the trails at Cuyuna.

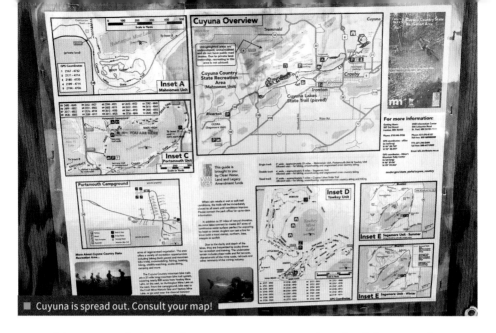

Cuyuna is spread out. Consult your map!

geocaching.com and sign up for an account. You can download the geocaching app and look for geocaches while you're on the trail.

If you prefer to start from the trailhead in Baxter, you can reach it by going from the intersection of MN 210 and MN 371 north one block to Excelsior Road, then east 0.75 mile to Conservation Drive. The parking lot is on the left. Merrifield is 9 miles from Baxter, with bathrooms at the Lion's shelter. Nisswa is 15 miles from Baxter (just south of town is Lake Hubert, a nice rest stop), and Pequot Lakes is about 21 miles. Information about the trail and a map can be found at dnr.state.mn.us /state_trails/paul_bunyan.

MOUNTAIN BIKING

If you're looking for something other than a leisurely ride, the star of this biking show is clearly the 25 miles of singletrack dirt mountain bike trails of the **Cuyuna Mountain Bike Trail System**, which offer a wide range of difficulty and have been designated Silver level by the International Mountain Biking Association.

The Miner's Mountain Rally Center, just north of Ironton, is a good place to start. To get to the center, instead of following MN 30 out of Ironton as you would to get to **Portsmouth Campground**, go left at the intersection where the highway goes right; you'll see a sign for the recreation area and the state bike trail between the two roads. Follow the road about 0.7 mile and then turn right. Huntington Mine Lake will be on your left. Parking is straight ahead. This is a good spot for a picnic and a view of the lake if you need a little sustenance before your ride.

The majority of the trails are north of Huntington Mine Lake, with some on the south side, but they can also be found adjacent to several other lakes, including Portsmouth Mine and Yawkey Mine.

In winter, the area grooms 40 miles of trail for fat biking, although bikers share the path with snowshoers and cross-country skiers (no hiking allowed). For a map of the mountain bike trails, go to files.dnr.state.mn.us/maps/state_parks/sra00302.pdf.

HIKING ⬤

You can hike the Cuyuna Lakes State Trail if you don't mind sharing it with the bikers. If you're going to stay at Crow Wing State Park, several miles of the paved Paul Bunyan State Trail are within park borders, but a better option for hiking is one of these trails:

Battle of 1786 Trail *2.3-mile loop*

This may win the award for trail name! The mostly grass-and-gravel trail leaves from the main parking lot and heads south along the Mississippi River to (and back from) the site of a major battle between the Dakota and Ojibwe tribes.

Hiking Club Trail *2.3 miles*

This trail, which sports a few hills, begins at the picnic shelter and offers plenty of historical spots. Follow the path (going clockwise) north along the river, where you'll see the Old Crow Wing Village site. You'll walk along a segment of the Red River Oxcart Trail, where you can still spot tracks from oxcarts that went through the area in the 1800s. You'll work your way back south and then east to the Chippewa Lookout, with great views of the river. Heading back south, you'll end up on a paved road going past the old Catholic and Lutheran sites before you end up back at the picnic shelter. (For information on the Hiking Club, see page 101.)

PADDLING ⊗

The beautiful, clean waters of the mine lakes in Cuyuna are filled with water so clear you can see down 40 feet, making them popular with paddlers, including an increasing number of stand-up paddleboarders. A good choice for paddling is the 46-acre **Pennington Mine Lake,** just northwest of Ironton, which you can access in a number of places, including near the Miner's Mountain Rally Center. Pennington provides paddlers easy access to five adjacent lakes. While there is also plenty of paddling on the big lakes in this area, including on Gull Lake and the Whitefish chain, when you paddle in the Cuyuna waters, there are no motorized vessels, big or small. Some people in the area say the experience is somewhat akin to paddling the Boundary Waters Canoe Area. I'm not sure I'd go that far, but it is nice—and there's no portaging.

If you find yourself wanting to paddle at Crow Wing State Park, it's easy to rent a canoe from the park office ($15 for a half day, $25 for a full day) and launch right in the park.

OTHER ADVENTURES ⊕/RAINY DAY ☻

Paul Bunyan Land *17553 MN 18, Brainerd; 218-764-2524; paulbunyanland.com; open Memorial Day weekend–Labor Day, daily, 10 a.m.–6 p.m.; admission is free for kids age 2 and younger, $21.95 for ages 3–64, and $18.95 for people age 65 and older.*

■ Kids still love to visit Babe.

OK, who doesn't want to see a 26-foot-tall talking animated lumberjack? That's what I thought. Visiting Paul Bunyan Land and being greeted by the big statue of Paul has been a rite of passage for Minnesota kids for generations. So what if it's a bit cheesy! Paul and Babe the Blue Ox, however, no longer reside between Brainerd and Baxter. For the last few years, they've been plying their trade at a facility about 8 miles east of Brainerd, having moved along with the Bunyan-themed attractions and amusement rides. There's also a pioneer village. Paul still greets kids by name, but I'm not telling you how. You'll have to visit to learn the trick.

Croft Mine Historical Park *N. 8th St. and 2nd Ave. E., Crosby; 218-546-5926; open Memorial Day weekend–Labor Day weekend, Saturdays, Sundays, and holidays, 10 a.m.–6 p.m.; free admission*

Without mining, the Cuyuna Country State Recreation Area wouldn't exist. The Croft Mine, which closed in 1934, had a shaft that went down 630 feet and produced high-quality iron ore. Here's a chance to see how it all worked. A guided tour takes you through the facility, which includes the original smokestack and the dry cage where the miners cleaned up after their work underground.

Pirate's Cove Adventure Golf and Billy Bones Raceway *17992–94 MN 371 N., Brainerd; 218-828-9002; piratescove.net, billybonesraceway.com*

Normally, I would not recommend minigolf as part of an adventure weekend (and you'll probably not want to do it on a rainy day). But just this once . . . because my kids have had plenty of good times at this place (well, me too). A fun, well-kept, pirate-themed, 36-hole course is the centerpiece of the place, but the Billy Bones Raceway next door is a blast too. The raceway has a variety of courses appropriate for all ages.

FOOD AND DRINK 🥛

The Barn *711 Washington St., Brainerd; 218-829-9297*

The Barn has been around since 1926. Does that tell you something? The restaurant is small, so there is occasionally a wait for seating, but if locals are willing to wait for their Maid-Rite sandwiches and homemade pies, you should be too. It's worth it. Open 7 a.m.–3 p.m.

Roundhouse Brewery *Northern Pacific Center, 1551 Northern Pacific Road, Brainerd; 218-454-2739; roundhousebrew.com*

When in Brainerd, this is a family favorite, and a couple of growlers always seem to make their way home from here. It's a nice setting, and there's a large and eclectic collection of brews to sample. The Golden Spike IPA is recommended, as is the Boom Lake lager. Want something really different? Try the Night Shift Coffee Stout, a full-bodied stout mixed with coffee from Reality Roasters in Little Falls.

A number of restaurants have sprung up in Crosby and Ironton to cater to folks visiting the Cuyuna Country State Recreation Area. Here are a few options:

North Country Cafe *12 W. Main St., Crosby; 218-545-9908; north-country-cafe.business.site*

Louie's Bucket of Bones *101 4th St., Ironton; 218-545-3232; sites.google.com/site/louiesbucketofbones*

Mixed Company–A Kava House *128 W. Main St., Crosby; 218-545-1010; enjoymixedcompany.com*

GEAR AND RESUPPLY 🛒

Red Raven Bike Café *2 3rd Ave. SW, Crosby; 218-833-2788; redraven.bike*

Is this a bike shop that sells food and drink, or a restaurant that sells bikes? I can't decide, but I do know it's a pretty cool place to grab an espresso, a sandwich, or even a glass of wine while getting a flat tire fixed. The folks here know bikes, whether they have fat tires or skinny ones, and they have plenty available for rent (or to buy) if you haven't brought your own.

Cycle Path & Paddle *115 3rd Ave. SW, Crosby; 218-545-4545; cyclepathpaddle.com*

This place has been around since 2005, an early supporter of Cuyuna as a biking destination. But besides bike rentals and sales, they can put you in a kayak, canoe, or stand-up paddleboard for the day or weekend. What's especially nice is their online reservation system, so you know you can get what you want for your trip even before you leave home.

Life Cycle *14843 Edgewood Drive, Baxter; 218-829-8542; ridelifecycle.com*

If you're riding the Paul Bunyan Trail or others in the Brainerd/Baxter area, here's your spot for sales and service. Life Cycle also provides rentals from its shop right off the trail in Nisswa (25336 Smiley Road, 218-963-0699) and, for Cuyuna riders, at 825 1st St. SW in Crosby.

Bear Head Lake State Park offers 14 miles of trails.

ELY

Ely is well known in Minnesota as the launching pad for many a canoe trip to the Boundary Waters Canoe Area (BWCA) Wilderness. But you don't have to dip a paddle in the wilderness to enjoy this part of the state. Two inviting Minnesota state parks are just a short distance from Ely—it's less than 20 minutes to either Bear Head Lake State Park or the campground at Lake Vermilion–Soudan Underground Mine State Park.

The campground at Lake Vermilion is the newest in the Minnesota system and a good example of the latest trends in Minnesota state parks. Bear Head Lake is the grizzled veteran in this scenario but gets our nod as the top pick for camping because of its distinctive north woods feel. Flip a coin—either is an appealing base camp for your outdoors weekend.

Areas included: Bear Head Lake State Park, Lake Vermilion–Soudan Underground Mine State Park, Ely, Soudan, International Wolf Center

Adventures: Camping, biking, hiking, paddling, exploring

Directions: To get to Bear Head Lake State Park from the Forest Lake area north of the Twin Cities, go about 109 miles north on I-35 and take Exit 237 to MN 33 in Cloquet. In about 19 miles take the ramp onto US 53, heading north. Drive about 48 miles, and north of Virginia, take the MN 169 exit toward Ely. Stay on MN 169 for about 30 miles, then turn right on Bear Head Lake State Park Road. The park will be about 4 miles ahead.

ELY

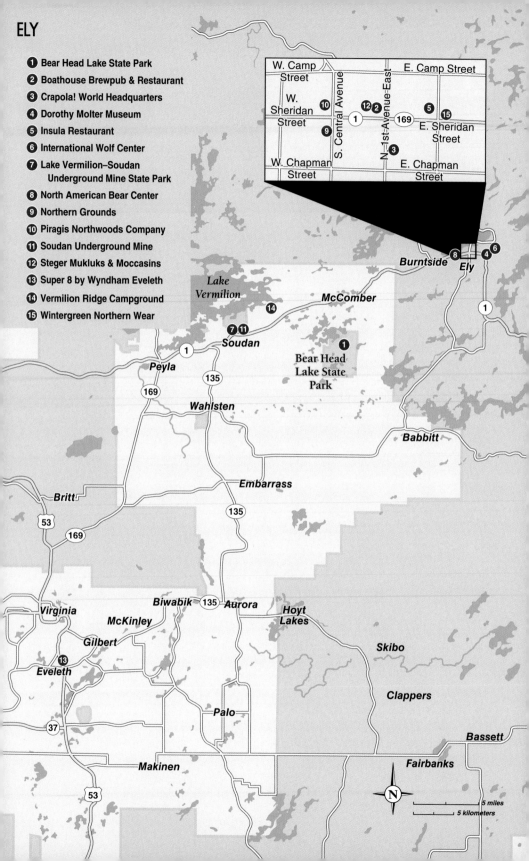

TOP PICK

BEAR HEAD LAKE STATE PARK (MINNESOTA DEPARTMENT OF NATURAL RESOURCES) *9301 Bear Head State Park Road; 218-235-2520; dnr.state.mn.us /state_parks/park.html?id=spk00109. $17–$23/night ($8 more for sites with electric hookups) for drive-in sites, 79 sites, 45 have electric hookups; $13–$15/night for backpack sites, 5 sites (1 site accessible only by boat or canoe); $60–$70/night for camper cabins, 5 cabins, electricity and heat in all cabins; reservations required; sites have picnic table, fire ring, grill, showers, flush and vault toilets; showers and flush toilets only available mid-May–end of September (check with park for specific dates); state park permit required ($35 annual, $7 daily).*

Bear Head Lake State Park, 16 miles southwest of Ely and about 4 hours from the Twin Cities, is a typical northern Minnesota state park, and I mean that in a good way. Its 4,000 acres are exactly what we visualize when we think of the north woods—pine, birch, and aspen trees, and lots of them. But the park is defined by its water as much as its land, highlighted by the 674-acre Bear Head Lake and its numerous bays.

Bear Head has only a few hiking trails, but they total 14 miles and will give you a workout. In winter, several miles are groomed for cross-country skiing. The park office rents canoes, kayaks, and paddleboards, which is nice at a park with this much water, as well as boats and motors for those interested in fishing. Snowshoes are available for rent in the winter.

The Bear Head Lake campground consists of two loops. The loop to the west has sites with electric hookups, and the loop to the east does not. If you've read any other chapters of the book, you'll know which one I prefer—the nonelectric loop. I do like that sites in both loops generally have plenty of woods behind and often to the sides, even if they are fairly open to the road. But the sites on the nonelectric loop have more space between, especially those on the outside of the loop. Overall, it's a very nice campground.

■ Many sites at Bear Head have a good buffer of woods for maximum privacy.

BACKUP BASE CAMP

Lake Vermilion–Soudan Underground Mine State Park (Minnesota Department of Natural Resources) *1302 McKinley Park Road, Soudan; 218-300-7000; dnr.state.mn.us /state_parks/park.html?id=spk00285. Camping at Lake Vermilion unit (Vermilion Ridge Campground) only; $25–$28/night for drive-in sites, all with electric hookups, 33 sites; $13–$15/night for backpack sites, 5 sites (1 site accessible only by boat or canoe); reservations required; sites have picnic table, fire ring, grill, showers, flush and vault toilets; showers only available mid-May–mid-October (check with park for specific dates); state park permit required ($35 annual, $7 daily).*

Welcome to the newest state park—sort of—in the Minnesota system. Soudan Underground Mine had been a Minnesota state park since the early 1960s, albeit without camping facilities. But the Lake Vermilion unit, about a mile from Soudan, opened in the fall of 2017 as part of Soudan, hence the new hyphenated name. The new combo is officially considered Minnesota's first new state park property since 1992. When the Lake Vermilion land, including 5 miles of shoreline, became available from U.S. Steel in 2010, the state jumped at the chance to add a recreational facility on one of Minnesota's most beautiful and iconic lakes. It took seven years for the planning and construction of campgrounds, three group camps, and a day-use area.

Lake Vermilion campsite

When it came to building the campground, the park opted to design the sites to be as friendly as possible to recreational vehicles. It's easy for them to maneuver in the campground, and 30- and 50-amp outlets are included at each site. But the outlets aren't just a concession to the growing use of RVs—they're an admission as well that, these days, many families are more attracted to parks where they can plug in electronic gear even if they are camping in tents. The campsites in the park are in a beautiful setting but are generally not very secluded. Many of the sites numbered in the 300s are very open to the road. In the loop with the sites numbered in the 400s, sites 402 and 404 are the nicest. There's a very small loop with sites numbered in the 200s; the northwest sites, 204 and 206, are the best ones there.

While the picnic facilities and group camps in the park are as nice as any in the state, there are as of yet no hiking trails here. They are planned, however, along with more campsites and up to eight camper cabins. For now, the primary recreation in the park will be Lake Vermilion fishing, and there are plenty of amenities for those interested in wetting a line.

Another unique facet of the park is that there is no staffed office, just information kiosks, a nod to the fact that all park reservations are done online or by phone. If you show up without a reservation, you can make one online or call from a phone at the campground entrance. Park rangers do make regular rounds through the park, checking reservations and handling questions. Firewood is available at the entrance to the campground, with a paybox attached to the wood shed (so make sure you have some cash with you).

> **Directions** Vermilion is about 6 miles east from Soudan, but most of that is the 4.5 miles between the Vermilion unit entrance on MN 169 and its campground.

INDOOR LODGING

You're not going to find much in the way of indoor lodging, other than that available in the park, within about 20 miles of Bear Head. Accommodations in nearby Ely range from bare-bones (often preferred by those setting out for BWCA trips) to fancy resort-style lodges. You can check them all out at ely.org/lodging/motels. If you want to go inexpensive here, in general you will find the motor inns better kept than in a lot of places. If you go the opposite direction from Ely, you'll have to drive some distance, but you will find a variety of chain hotels along the main drag in Virginia. Or, if you don't mind the drive, keep going to Eveleth, which has probably the finest Super 8 in the entire chain.

Super 8 by Wyndham *1080 Industrial Park Drive, Eveleth; 218-297-0782; wyndhamhotels .com/super-8/eveleth-minnesota/super-8-eveleth/overview; $109–$159/night*

This Super 8 has made a trade-off. It charges more than most of the hotels in this chain, but the local owners pride themselves in a facility much nicer than the rest. The rooms are clean and well maintained, but what makes a difference at this place is the extra-nice lobby and sitting area, seasonally decorated, and the better-than-average breakfast room.

HIKING ○

Besides the 14 miles of trails in Bear Head Lake State Park, you can take the Cub Lake Spur Trail for about a mile northwest out of the park to hook up with the **Taconite State Trail**, which goes 165 miles from Grand Rapids to Ely. Most of the trail is natural surface used for snowmobiling in the winter months, but it's good for hiking as well during the warmer part of the year. There's a nice little stretch that goes from the Cub Lake Trail intersection to the edge of Eagle Nest Lake No. Three. A map of the trail, with more information about it, can be found at files.dnr.state.mn.us/maps /state_trails/arrowhead_taconite.pdf.

If you stay in the park, here are a couple of hiking options:

Hiking Club Trail *3-mile loop*

The Hiking Club Trail is also called the Norberg Lake Loop, and while it's not long, it is hilly and rugged. The trail starts at the beach/picnic area. If you take it counterclockwise, the trail heads along the northern side of East Bay Lake, going northeast until it turns south toward the group camp. The trail heads northeast again and then west past Norberg Lake. You'll turn south near the parking area and park office, and then it's straight to the end. (For information on the Hiking Club, see page 101.)

Becky Lake and Blueberry Lake Trails *About 3 or about 4.5 miles*

There's a parking area north of Norberg Lake or one west of the lake for backpack campsite parking. Taking the Becky Lake Trail loop counterclockwise will lead you past a spur to a backpack/watercraft campsite on the southeastern edge of East Bay Lake and then around to a backpack site on Becky Lake. You then have a choice—head back north on Becky Lake Trail, or add in the 1.6-mile Blueberry Lake Trail loop, which will take you past three backpacking campsites. It then heads back to Becky for the completion of the loop.

BIKING

Mesabi Bike Trail

The Mesabi Trail is a long-distance bike path that passes by the Soudan Mine portion of Lake Vermilion–Soudan Underground Mine State Park, and then continues to Lake Vermilion. It's a nice ride from one to the other, about 8 miles between Soudan and Lake Vermilion, if you go all the way to the terminus east of the Lake Vermilion campground. The full trail is still under construction, with about 135 miles of a planned 155-mile route complete as of late 2018. You can find a hodgepodge of trail maps online, including at mesabitrail.com, but the information can be outdated. I've found if you call the trail information number at 877-637-2241, you'll get someone helpful who can give you the current status of the trail construction.

For access to the trail near Soudan, go from the mine area to MN 169 and turn left. In a few blocks you'll turn north into Breitung Monument Park. Parking and restrooms are located in the park. You can also access the trail from Tower, which is west of Soudan, by turning south onto Pine Street; parking is available at the Civic Center, and trail access is located two blocks away.

■ The trails at Bear Head Lake State Park will give you a workout.

OTHER ADVENTURES ⊕/RAINY DAY 😎

International Wolf Center *1396 MN 169, Ely; 218-365-4695; wolf.org; admission is $7 for children ages 4–12, $13 for adults, and $11 for seniors.*

If you're lucky when camping in this area of the state, you might hear the howl of a wolf. But your best chance to see one is at the International Wolf Center. There are usually about four wolves in a live exhibit. They're fascinating to observe, and you might learn a thing or two. A beautiful facility houses plenty of educational exhibits as well. This is pretty much an essential stop when in the Ely area.

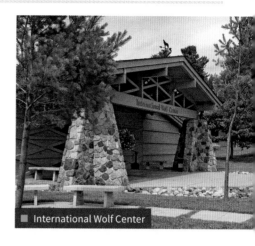

■ International Wolf Center

> ***Directions*** The International Wolf Center is about 18 miles from Bear Head Lake State Park. Exit the park and in about 4 miles turn right on MN 169. Take MN 169 13.6 miles through Ely to the wolf center.

Soudan Underground Mine *1302 McKinley Park Road, Soudan; 218-300-7000; dnr.state .mn.us/state_parks/lake_vermilion_soudan/tours.html; admission is $10 for children ages 5–12 and $15 for adults; reservations can be made in advance at reservemn.usedirect.com /MinnesotaWeb/Activities/programsandtours.aspx.*

It's well worth a visit to Minnesota's first iron ore mine for the 90-minute tour, which takes you in a cage a half mile underground. Once at the bottom, you'll ride a rail car for about 0.75 mile while a guide tells you the history of the operation. The mine, which produced ore that was used to make high-quality steel, was closed in 1962. It's a constant 51°F in the mine, so dress warmly.

> ***Directions from Bear Head Lake State Park*** The mine is about 12 miles west from Bear Head Lake State Park. Exit the park and in about 4 miles turn left on MN 169. Take MN 169 7.5 miles and turn right on Main Street. In about 500 feet continue onto McKinley Park Road. In 0.3 mile turn right to continue on McKinley, and the mine will be ahead.

North American Bear Center *1926 MN 169, Ely; 218-365-7879; bear.org; admission is $8 for children ages 3–8, $13 for teens and adults, and $12 for seniors; open mid-April–late October (check for specific dates).*

The center has a wealth of bear-related exhibits and programs, plus a 2.5-acre forested enclosure with four bears that can be viewed through glass or from a balcony. It's definitely more fun to see a bear here than in your campsite!

> ***Directions from Bear Head Lake State Park*** The bear center is about 15 miles from Bear Head Lake State Park. Take the park road out, and in about 4 miles turn right on MN 169. Take MN 169 11.4 miles toward Ely to the bear center.

Dorothy Molter Museum *2002 E. Sheridan St., Ely; 218-365-4451; rootbeerlady.com; admission is $4.50 for youth ages 6–17, $6.50 for adults, and $6 for seniors; guided tours are optional.*

Dorothy Molter is a Minnesota legend. She was the longtime operator of the Pines Resort and became famous for her root beer—she was, and is, the Root Beer Lady. Molter was an accomplished outdoors person, and, other than for her root beer, may be best known for being allowed to stay in her cabin when the property became part of the BWCA. She lived there until she died in 1986. The highlight of the museum property is Molter's winter cabin, which has her original root beer brewing equipment.

> **Directions from Bear Head Lake State Park** The museum is about 18 miles from Bear Head Lake State Park. Take the park road out, and in about 4 miles turn right on MN 169. Take MN 169 13.6 miles to Ely and continue straight onto E. Sheridan Street. The museum will be 0.4 mile ahead on your left.

FOOD AND DRINK

Northern Grounds *2 W. Sheridan St., Ely; 218-235-6162; thenortherngrounds.com*

I've always thought of Northern Grounds as the best place for a great coffee drink in Ely. But they've expanded their repertoire over the years to include an excellent selection of wines and craft brews. If you need a gluten-free option, as my wife does, try the excellent Burning Brothers Pale Ale.

Crapola! World Headquarters *16 N. 1st Ave., Ely; 218-235-6161; crapola.us*

You know what Crapola! is, right? The mixture of cranberries, apples, and granola? No? Well, now you do. But the best way to understand its goodness is to stop by their little café and try it. The stuff has a cult following. The café serves parfaits, smoothies, coffee and juice drinks, and sourdough breads.

Boathouse Brewpub & Restaurant *47 E. Sheridan St., Ely; 218-365-4301; boathousebrewpub.com*

This has been a go-to restaurant during Ely trips for years. They do some unique takes on the burger and have a very interesting sandwich that puts walleye and cheddar cheese on rye. Wow. To top it off, they brew their own beer, available for takeout in growlers.

Insula Restaurant *145 E. Sheridan St., Ely; 218-365-4855; insularestaurant.com*

Insula is a relative newcomer to Ely, opening in 2015, but has quickly built a reputation for a higher level of cuisine (and service) than is usually found in a small town, with an emphasis on local sourcing. For breakfast, the ricotta pancakes are amazing, and they have a nice pot pie for dinner. I particularly like the northern pike sandwich; most restaurants only serve walleye, but the pike tastes every bit as good (I think) and is far less expensive.

GEAR AND RESUPPLY 🛒

In some chapters of this book, we struggle to find decent places near your campground where you can pick up forgotten supplies or gear. That's not an issue here—Ely is full of incredible outfitters who cater to BWCA trippers. And it's just a lot of fun to wander up and down the streets of Ely. If you can't find what you need in Ely, you don't really need it.

Piragis Northwoods Company *105 N. Central Ave., Ely; 218-365-6745; piragis.com*

Local legend Steve Piragis has built a big business through his Boundary Waters Catalog, and you can find most of what's in there in his retail operation in Ely. Just be warned—if you're not careful, you'll walk in for a water bottle or stove fuel and not emerge for hours. There's a lot of cool stuff in here, from camping gear to outdoors clothing to a full line of paddling gear and canoes.

Steger Mukluks & Moccasins *33 E. Sheridan St., Ely; 218-365-3322; mukluks.com*

Patti Steger, once married to Arctic explorer Will Steger, has been making winter footwear out of Ely since 1985 and now produces more than 14,000 pairs of mukluks and moccasins a year. It's fascinating to browse the different kinds of boots in this nice little shop, and although you may not need a pair of mukluks on your summer camping trip, you may end up going home with a pair anyway. My wife and daughter did, and they've worn them as their winter footwear of choice ever since.

Wintergreen Northern Wear *205 E. Sheridan St., Ely; 218-365-6602;*
wintergreennorthernwear.com

Paul Schurke is almost as well known for Arctic exploration as Will Steger is—they were the coleaders of the famous 1986 unsupported dogsled expedition to the North Pole. So he knows a little something about cold-weather clothing. After operating the business for years, Susan and Paul Schurke sold it in 2009, but the new owners closed shop four years later and the Schurkes have been back at the helm with their original designs since 2015. They offer distinctively patterned anoraks, jackets, pants, and other outdoor clothing, all made in Ely.

■ The main drag in Ely

The falls at Cascade River State Park

GRAND MARAIS

The North Shore of Lake Superior offers way too many recreational opportunities to cover in one chapter, so we've broken it into bite-size chunks, starting here with Grand Marais; you'll find later chapters on Silver Bay and Two Harbors. This is a good one to start with because, for many Minnesotans, Grand Marais is synonymous with the North Shore. That may be surprising to anyone who hasn't been there, as Grand Marais isn't the biggest community on the lake and it's a 5-hour drive from the Twin Cities—90 miles past Two Harbors, the first significant destination on the shore.

So what is it about Grand Marais? First, there's the beauty—a scenic harbor on one side and the Sawtooth Mountains on the other. Then there's the proximity to outdoor adventure; the Gunflint Trail, a main entry to the Boundary Waters Canoe Area, begins here, but there are countless hiking, biking, and paddling opportunities as well. It also helps that Grand Marais, with an area of less than 3 square miles, has worked fiercely to maintain its small-town charm. Take advantage of the eclectic mix of goods and services in town to ensure you're well supplied for your activities, then head out for the nearby outdoor adventures of your choice. When you return, you can explore the wealth of options for food and drink as you wait for the call of the sleeping bag.

Areas included: Grand Marais, Cascade River State Park, Superior Hiking Trail (SHT), Lake Superior, Superior National Forest, Pincushion Mountain, Eagle Mountain

Adventures: Camping, biking, hiking, exploring, paddling, backpacking

Directions: Grand Marais is 235 miles from Forest Lake, north of the Twin Cities. Take I-35 north from Forest Lake about 128 miles. In Duluth, turn right on MN 61 (London Road) and continue about 107 miles to Grand Marais. (You can also take the North Shore Scenic Drive, the old MN 61 between Duluth and Two Harbors, which will add a bit of time to your trip but will give you plenty of views of Lake Superior and some nice places to stop. You can choose that route as you reach the northeast edge of Duluth.)

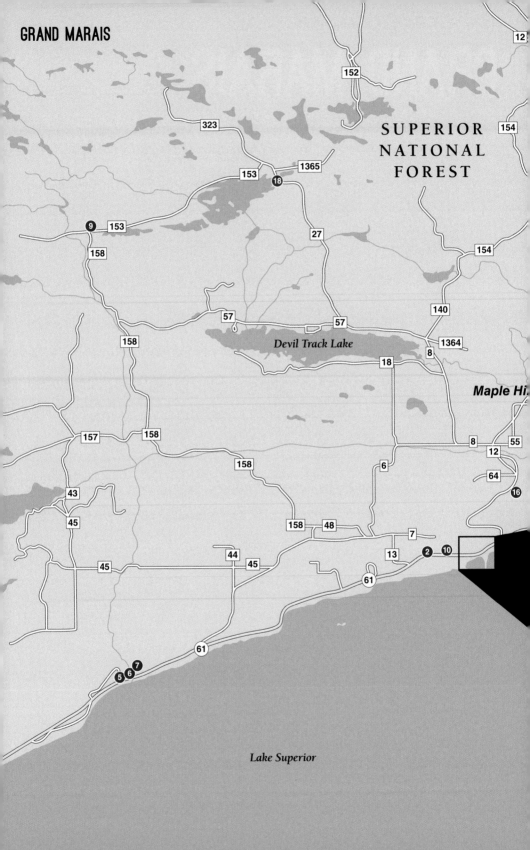

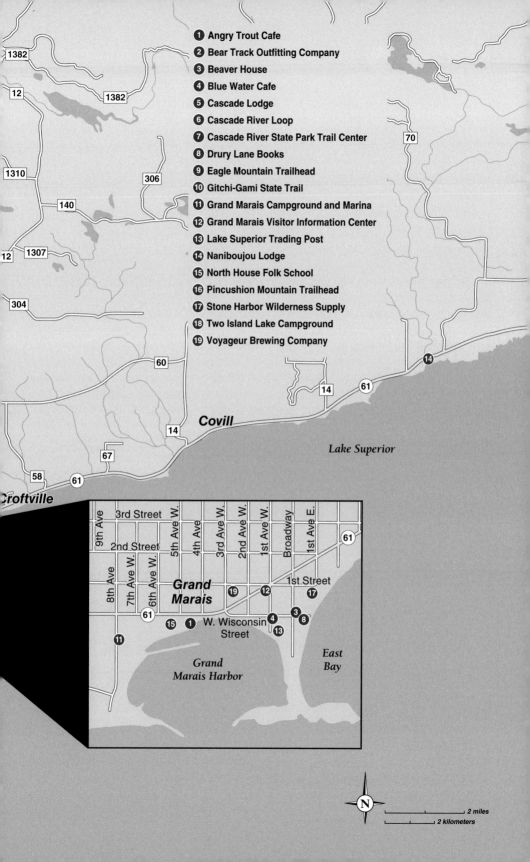

1 Angry Trout Cafe
2 Bear Track Outfitting Company
3 Beaver House
4 Blue Water Cafe
5 Cascade Lodge
6 Cascade River Loop
7 Cascade River State Park Trail Center
8 Drury Lane Books
9 Eagle Mountain Trailhead
10 Gitchi-Gami State Trail
11 Grand Marais Campground and Marina
12 Grand Marais Visitor Information Center
13 Lake Superior Trading Post
14 Naniboujou Lodge
15 North House Folk School
16 Pincushion Mountain Trailhead
17 Stone Harbor Wilderness Supply
18 Two Island Lake Campground
19 Voyageur Brewing Company

Covill

Lake Superior

Croftville

Grand Marais

3rd Street
2nd Street
1st Street
W. Wisconsin Street

9th Ave
8th Ave
7th Ave W.
6th Ave W.
5th Ave W.
4th Ave
3rd Ave W.
2nd Ave W.
1st Ave W.
Broadway
1st Ave E.

Grand Marais Harbor

East Bay

N

2 miles
2 kilometers

TOP PICK

TWO ISLAND LAKE CAMPGROUND (U.S. FOREST SERVICE) *Ball Club Road, Grand Marais; 218-626-4300; fs.usda.gov/recarea/superior/recarea/?recid=37017. $16–$18/ night for drive-in sites, 38 sites, no reservations required; sites have picnic table, fire ring, grill, food storage boxes, vault toilets, water, no showers, picnic area.*

U.S. Forest Service campgrounds in Minnesota are hidden treasures. They offer most of the amenities of state parks, but because they lack showers and electrical hookups, they are rarely as busy. (You can go a weekend without a shower, can't you?) Forest Service campgrounds also don't take reservations, which makes them a good choice if you've decided to pitch your tent at the last minute and the state parks are full.

The best thing about Two Island is it provides a rustic setting for your camp only minutes from Grand Marais, and it's a beautiful little campground to boot. It's nice and small with only 38 campsites, and there is plenty of privacy. A few sites do sit close to the road, so if you're looking for maximum seclusion, take a spin around the park and look for one of the sites that has a short set of stairs that go down to the tent pad—it might add a bit to your setup, but the effort is worth it. The sites numbered in the 30s are the most remote, and closest to the lake, with paths that will take you from your tent right to the water.

Directions From Grand Marais, take MN 61 and turn north on 5th Avenue West, which is the same as County Road 12 (Gunflint Trail). Go north about 4 miles to CR 8. Turn west and continue about 6 miles to CR 27. Go northwest on CR 27 (Ball Club Road) and continue 4 miles to the campground entrance.

■ Campsites at Two Island Lake are private and spacious.

BACKUP BASE CAMP

Grand Marais Campground and Marina (private) *MN 61 and 8th Ave. W., Grand Marais; 218-387-1712; grandmaraisrecreationarea.com; $19–$55/night, including $27/night on weekends for wooded tent sites and $32/night on weekends for lakeside tent sites, $40 deposit required at reservation; open year-round, with some amenities only available seasonally; 300 sites, including 57 primitive sites with lake views of wooded privacy, reservations recommended, picnic table, firebox, flush toilets, water, hot showers.*

A municipal campground is usually not the first choice for an adventure weekend, and while it might be a bit of a stretch to call staying at the Grand Marais Campground and Marina a wilderness experience, this park does have tent-only areas that will keep you away from the RVs, and the sites are nicely wooded. If Two Island seems too far from town, this campground will put you within walking distance of downtown.

The campground has 26 tent-only sites that include a fire pit and picnic table, with vault toilets and water spigots nearby. If you're looking for a secluded, wooded site, go for those numbered in the 200s.

INDOOR LODGING

Grand Marais and nearby environs boast the largest number of lodging options on the North Shore, from basic hotel rooms to grand resorts. You can find a list at north shorevisitor.com. But the way we see it, if you're going someplace like Grand Marais, you're cheating yourself by staying in a generic hotel room. Go for something unique!

Cascade Lodge *3719 W. MN 61, Lutsen; 218-387-1112; cascadelodgemn.com; $99–$299/ night, rooms and suites in main lodge, motel rooms, cabins, and chalet*

Cascade Lodge, in business since 1927, is about 10 minutes southwest of Grand Marais on MN 61. (Its Lutsen address is deceiving.) The lodge's proximity to the Cascade River and Lake Superior, with numerous outdoor activities just steps away, is what wins it a place here. The charm of the property, as well as the wonderful restaurant and pub across the driveway, makes it even better. The Cascade has been a favorite of my family since we first started going to the North Shore more than two decades ago. There is a spur trail that leads 0.3 mile from the lodge to the Superior Hiking Trail at Cascade River State Park (see pages 66–67).

Naniboujou Lodge *20 Naniboujou Trail, Grand Marais; 218-387-2688; naniboujou.com; $110–$135/night; open May–October, Thanksgiving week, and some winter weekends (check with lodge for specific dates)*

It's pretty safe to say there's nowhere else on the North Shore you could stay where Babe Ruth and Jack Dempsey slept before you! The Naniboujou, 15 minutes northeast of Grand Marais, is one of the most historic structures on the lake. It started out as a private club in the 1920s (with Ruth and Dempsey as members), but it failed after the Great Depression and was opened to the public as a hotel in 1939. Its architecture includes the largest stone fireplace in the state, as well as the dining room's stunning walls and ceiling, painted by the French artist Antoine Gouffee. This is the place to go if you really want to unplug—there are no phones or TVs in the rooms, no Wi-Fi, and only spotty cell coverage.

Because of the proximity of the Superior Hiking Trail and several state parks, hiking opportunities abound in the Grand Marais area. The abundance of trails does make it easy to get off on a wrong segment, so before you head out, double-check to make sure you have your map with you. (You always carry a map anyway, right? You should!)

Here are some options:

Pincushion Mountain Trailhead to Devil Track River and County Road 58 *4.9 miles, requires two cars or shuttle*

This section includes the A-frame bridge that spans Devil Track River, one of the iconic structures on the SHT. Beginning at the trailhead parking lot, the SHT shares a ski and mountain biking trail for just over 2 miles. At the 0.4-mile mark, the trail goes right, heading through woods and crossing a number of streams. At 1.7 miles, take the spur trail to the summit of Pincushion Mountain; it's a steep trek for a quar-

■ Above Grand Marais

ter of a mile, but you're rewarded with spectacular views of Grand Marais and Lake Superior. When you get back on the main trail, go 0.5 mile to the junction where the SHT splits from the ski trail, and descend to the river, where you'll be glad you were going down and not up. In the next half mile, you'll encounter two of the most coveted backpacking campsites on the entire trail. You'll cross the river between them on the 50-foot A-frame bridge. Stop for a look and consider the difficulty of building such a structure way back in the woods. (Hint: it took helicopters!)

The trail climbs after the second campsite, crossing bridges at 2.9 and 3.5 miles. Keep your eyes open for waterfalls. There's another nice view at Barrier Falls overlook, before you drop to a stream crossing. You'll hike through mixed forest before hitting the CR 58/Lindskog Road trailhead.

Please note that we rate this stretch moderate, but that is an average. The southern half is relatively easy as it follows a ski trail, but the northern half is fairly strenuous.

> **Directions** At MN 61 mile marker 110, turn north on CR 12 (Gunflint Trail) and go 2 miles. Turn right on CR 53 (Pincushion Drive) and go about 0.25 mile to the parking lot.

Cascade River Loop *7.8 miles, state park and Superior Hiking Trail*

The Cascade River tumbles down 17 miles from the north to MN 61 between Grand Marais and Lutsen, carving out a rugged, dazzling landscape. The hiking trails that run on both sides of the river (some built by the Civilian Conservation Corps camp in the 1930s) offer scenic views in exchange for an often-challenging up-and-down trek, and the numerous waterfalls are some of the finest on the North Shore.

The entrance to **Cascade River State Park** is about 9 miles southwest of Grand Marais on MN 61, but to access the Cascade River Loop, you'll go another mile south down 61, where the river crosses under the road and flows into Lake Superior. There is parking available on both sides of the highway here (no overnight parking allowed).

To start the loop, take the trail from the parking lot on the north side of the highway about 0.25 mile (you'll be on the west side of

■ Looking down on the Cascade River

the river) until you reach a bridge, where you will have a great view of The Cascades waterfalls. Cross the bridge to the east side of the river and go left on the SHT, which will wind around and lead steeply to Trout Creek.

This used to be an SHT main trail, but it was redesignated a spur trail when the bridge over Trout Creek washed away. Even without the bridge, the creek is generally easy to cross. If it's not, or you're not comfortable with a water crossing, you'll have to turn around and rethink your hiking choice for the day. The reason it's recommended you hike this loop counterclockwise is that it's better to find out the status of Trout Creek at the beginning rather than near the end. If you do turn around, you could always hike up the west side of the river—just don't cross the bridge at the beginning—and go back down the same way.

If you continue on, at the 1-mile mark you'll reach the SHT's Trout Creek Campsite. The trail then follows a bluff, offering nice views, and eventually descends to the river at the 3.2-mile mark. You have one more good climb before you head back down and reach the bridge on CR 45. If you haven't taken a good break yet, now is the time! Once you're rested up, walk about a third of a mile west across the bridge and watch for the SHT sign on the left. A little tricky descent from the road—watch your footing—puts you back on the SHT, with just over 3.5 miles on the west side of the river to get back to MN 61. You'll run into Cut Long Campsite at the 2.3-mile mark, then the Big White Pine Campsite with 1.8 miles to go. Before you get back to the parking lot, you will again pass The Cascades and another set of waterfalls that you can view more closely by walking down a short spur trail.

One of the real highlights of the Cascade River Loop is the view of **The Cascades**, a series of five small waterfalls that is one of the most popular attractions in the park. If you don't have time to do the loop but want to see the falls, the best way is to drive into Cascade River State Park (permit required), go about 1 mile into the campground, and leave your vehicle near the trail center (don't confuse it with the visitor center near the park entrance). From there, follow the signs to the bridge over the river and a viewing platform, a walk of about 0.5 mile.

Directions to trailhead The trail starts at the parking lot near mile marker 100 on MN 61.

■ Lake Superior shimmers in the distance.

Eagle Mountain *7 miles*

If you're staying at Two Island Lake Campground, you're only about 5 miles from the trailhead to Eagle Mountain, the highest point in Minnesota (at an elevation of 2,301 feet). Standing on the highest spot in any state is always fun! Because it is within the Boundary Waters Canoe Area (BWCA) Wilderness, the route to the apex is designated as a wilderness trail, which means it will be a bit narrower and rockier than a pathway you might hike in a state park. Still, the 3.5-mile hike to the summit is only moderately difficult until about 0.5 mile from the end, when it begins to get a bit steep. *Note:* Because portions of the trail are in the BWCA, you'll need a day permit, which is free; there's a box at the trailhead where you can fill out the necessary paperwork.

Directions From Two Island Lake Campground, go northwest on Ball Club Road. Turn west on CR 153 (The Grade) and drive 4.9 miles until you reach the trailhead, near the intersection with CR 158 (Bally Creek Road).

Note: If you're starting your hike in one spot and ending in another, and you don't have vehicles you can leave at either end, there are options. The Superior Hiking Shuttle (218-834-5511, superiorhikingshuttle.com) operates on a schedule that is available online. You can plan to arrive at your hiking terminus in time to meet the shuttle and take it back to your starting point. But that puts pressure on you to stay on course, and the last thing you want in the woods is to have to adhere to a specific schedule. Here's a better idea: drive to where you want to end your hike, leave your vehicle, and pick up the shuttle there. Take it to the other end, start your hike, and head back toward your vehicle on your own schedule.

You can also use Harriet Quarles Transportation (218-370-9164 or 218-387-1801). Quarles doesn't work on a fixed timetable, so she can accommodate individual schedules, but you will need to call her to check availability and make reservations.

BIKING

ROAD BIKING

In 2017 The Minnesota Department of Transportation designated a route between the state's capital in Saint Paul and the Canadian border—a distance of 315 miles—as **U.S. Bicycle Route 41** (aka the **North Star Route**). This route goes right along MN 61, through Grand Marais.

But there's a difference between designating a route and building one. Most of the road biking you can do in this area is on the highway. There is a 2-mile segment of the **Gitchi-Gami State Trail** (ggta.org) from the western end of Grand Marais to the downtown area that will keep you off the highway. It's hardly enough to break a sweat, obviously, but at least you're not dodging traffic. (There are plans to connect that stretch to the Cut Face Creek wayside rest area about 4 miles to the west.) Otherwise, road biking is right along MN 61. If you're okay with highway riding, avoid the busier stretch of 61 south of Grand Marais—on the northern side of town, you'll find wider shoulders and less traffic.

A map of the Gitchi-Gami route can be found online at dnr.state.mn.us/maps /state_trails/gitchi_gami.pdf. An interactive map is also available at ggta.org/map.php.

MOUNTAIN BIKING

Pincushion Mountain *Seven trails, 0.5–2 miles each*

In the immediate Grand Marais area, your closest options for off-road biking are the Pincushion Mountain bike trails. They are narrow, hard-packed trails that lack long distance but climb enough to provide a challenge for even those with advanced skills. Maps of the seven trails can be found at superiorcycling.org/trails.

> *Directions* At MN 61 mile marker 110, turn north on CR 12 (Gunflint Trail) and go 2 miles. Turn right on CR 53 (Pincushion Drive) and go about 0.25 mile to the parking lot.

Devil Track/Bally Creek *24 miles*

Another choice if you're looking for more distance is the Devil Track/Bally Creek ride, which is on hard-packed gravel roads. It's not a loop, so you'll need two cars for shuttling if you don't ride it out and back.

> *Directions* Start at the Eagle Mountain trailhead parking lot. Ride down CR 158 (Bally Creek Road) about 5 miles to CR 157 (Cascade River Road), go west on 157 for 2 miles, and then turn south. Take CR 43 (North Pike Lake Road) southeast 0.5 mile to CR 45 (Pike Lake Road). Take CR 45 south 1.7 miles, turn east, and go 5 miles to CR 7. Take CR 7 northeast back into Grand Marais.

■ Grand Marais Harbor

PADDLING ⊗

The Minnesota Department of Natural Resources has established a Lake Superior water trail (dnr.state.mn.us/watertrails /lswt), intended primarily for kayakers, that you can access near the Coast Guard Station in the Grand Marais Harbor, as well as near the municipal campground. While bays and inlets along the route allow for leisurely paddling in good weather, this is Lake Superior, the largest freshwater lake in the world by surface area, and conditions can get treacherous. This is not a place to climb into a kayak for the first time unless you're content staying close to shore in a protected area (such as where the paddleboarders would be).

For a map of the water trail between the Caribou River and Grand Marais, visit dnr.state.mn.us/watertrails/lswt/three.html. A map of the trail from Grand Marais to the Pigeon River can be found at dnr.state.mn.us/watertrails/lswt/four.html.

NORTHERN LIGHTS

Minnesota is a great place to view the northern lights or, as they are officially known, the aurora borealis. The state is pretty much the southernmost location that offers consistent opportunities to see the lights, but it's virtually impossible if you're anywhere with light pollution—which includes population areas large and small.

However, if you're going places highlighted in this book, you're likely to be in locations much of the time that will be dark enough to see the lights—when they are out.

The long days of summer cut into viewing time, so your best chance is with the really dark skies after 11 p.m. or so. (Lights actually appear more frequently in the winter.) You'll need clear skies, preferably with a new moon or close to it, and a good view to the north. While the lights can be seen overhead in many locations, that doesn't happen much in Minnesota; your best chance to see them is right above the horizon.

Then all you need is cooperation from the atmosphere! The solar disturbances that create the lights are extremely difficult to forecast accurately, and even when conditions look like they are going to be exactly right, they can change at a moment's notice. Months can pass between the lights' appearance, or they can show up for several evenings in a row. Figuring out the language used for predictions is not easy, but a good place to start is by checking out the website at aurora-service.org. In addition, a number of Facebook groups actively report conditions, and if the lights are coming out, or have already appeared, you can find out at facebook.com/groups/greatlakesaurorahunters.

By the way, when you're looking for the lights, keep your expectations low. I have seen stunning, swirling shows with my naked eye, but just as often have seen only faint vertical pillars of light. Remember that most photos you see of the lights come from exposures of 20–30 seconds, allowing the camera to capture a lot more light than your eyes can.

The North Shore may actually be the best place to see the lights in Minnesota, and several chapters of this book take you there. For good viewing locations on the North Shore, check out visitcookcounty.com/adventures/northern-lights. Also, the Blue Hill Trail parking lot at the Sherburne National Wildlife Refuge, noted in the Lake Maria chapter, is another good spot for seeing the lights.

RAINY DAY 😎

Grand Marais is, without a doubt, the quintessential rainy day getaway on the North Shore. But even if the weather is good, you can mix both indoor and outdoor activities if you want to spend a day (or part of one) in town.

Grand Marais Visitor Information Center *116 W. MN 61, Grand Marais; 888-922-5000*

Drury Lane Books *12 E. Wisconsin St., Grand Marais; 218-387-3370; drurylanebooks.com*

Beaver House *3 E. Wisconsin St., Grand Marais; 218-387-3349*

You can't miss the place with the fish head sticking out of it! The Beaver House is where the popular Beaver Flick fishing lure was invented, but you don't have to be an angler to enjoy a tour of this iconic Grand Marais shop.

North House Folk School *500 W. MN 61, Grand Marais; 218-387-9762; northhouse.org*

The popular school teaches traditional northern crafts such as boat-building, basketry, and fiber art, bringing in instructors from around the world. Tours of the school are offered on Saturdays at 2 p.m. year-round, at no charge. There is also a school store, open daily, 8 a.m.–5 p.m.

■ The iconic Beaver House has been in business for over 50 years.

Want to stay outdoors? Park at the Grand Marais Coast Guard Station and walk toward Lake Superior. Turning left will take you out to scenic **Artist's Point.** Turning right will take you to the **Grand Marais Lighthouse.**

FOOD AND DRINK 🍔

Angry Trout Cafe *408 W. MN 61, Grand Marais; 218-387-1265; angrytroutcafe.com; open May–October for lunch and dinner (check for specific dates)*

Of all the must-visit places in Grand Marais, the Angry Trout may be at the top of the list. And there's a good reason why parking outside can sometimes be hard to come by—terrific food in a beautifully rustic converted fishing shanty. Locally sourced herring, whitefish, and—of course—lake trout in various forms are at the heart of the menu. A favorite is the smoked trout fettuccine; for lunch, try the Lake Superior fish-and-chips. On top of it all, the owners are committed to sustainable business practices, including serving organically and sustainably raised foods and relying on local providers for most of their menu.

If it's a nice day, consider dining outside at the Angry Trout Cafe.

Blue Water Cafe *20 Wisconsin St., Grand Marais; 218-387-1597; bluewatercafe.com*

The Blue Water is as close as you'll get to a classic diner in Grand Marais, and it plays the part well. The heart of any good diner is breakfast, and the Swedish pancakes and omelets here are excellent. At other times of day, try the beef pot roast or walleye sandwich, and if there's still room, homemade pie or bread pudding.

Voyageur Brewing Company *233 W. MN 61, Grand Marais; 218-387-3163; voyageurbrewing.com*

This is a brewery and taproom in the same place, offering seasonal craft beers and weekend tours of the brewery.

GEAR AND RESUPPLY 🛒

Lake Superior Trading Post *10 S. 1st Ave. W., Grand Marais; 218-387-2020; lakesuperiortradingpost.com*

OK, we'll say it right up front—we never go to Grand Marais without stopping at the trading post, whether we need anything or not. It has a great selection of gear and clothing. Best of all, it's right on the water, and Java Moose has an outpost on the premises, so you can enjoy a cup of coffee and watch the waves when you're done shopping.

Stone Harbor Wilderness Supply *22 E. 1st St., Grand Marais; 218-387-3136; stoneharborws.com*

Find supplies and equipment for purchase or rent, plus four-season guided tours.

Bear Track Outfitting Company *2011 W. MN 61, Grand Marais; 218-387-1162; bear-track.com*

Here's a great place to pick up any food you might have forgotten for your camping trip, plus equipment and gear for purchase and rent.

For some downtime, hit the beach at Grand Marais Harbor.

Fall is a beautiful time for hiking at Lake Maria.

LAKE MARIA

Lake Maria State Park is less than an hour's drive away for nearly three-quarters of Minnesota's population, including the Twin Cities. So why is this true treasure of the state park system among the most overlooked parks for Minnesota campers?

With only 17 campsites, Lake Maria (pronounced "muh-RYE-uh") is among the smallest in the state system, but the main factor is that Maria's sites are for back-packing only; except for a couple of group spots, there's no drive-in camping at Maria. Notice, however, I said the campsites are for *backpacking* . . . not that you had to be a *backpacker* to use them. Because many of the sites at Maria require a hike of only a few minutes, they are perfect for people who want to dip their toe in the water without committing to a total backpacking experience. Many people who camp at Maria possess not a single piece of backpacking gear, at least the first time they go out. It's easy to load your car-camping kit into a couple of duffel bags or a plastic bin for the walk in—although, until you realize that you really don't need a 55-quart cooler for an overnighter, it might take a couple of trips.

If you haven't experienced this kind of camping before, being away from the security blanket of a vehicle may seem daunting. For many people, though, the trepidation turns into a love affair with the solitude of the deep woods that simply can't be found in a traditional campground. There's only one way to find out if that could happen to you.

Areas included: Lake Maria State Park, Sand Dunes State Forest, Ann Lake Campground, Sherburne National Wildlife Refuge, Monticello

Adventures: Camping, biking, hiking, exploring, skiing

Directions: From the Twin Cities, take I-94 west to Monticello and turn off on MN 25 S at Exit 193. In 0.4 mile turn right on Chelsea Road, then in 1.4 miles turn left on County Road 39. Follow the road 5.4 miles and turn right on Clementa Avenue NW. The park will be 0.2 mile ahead on your left.

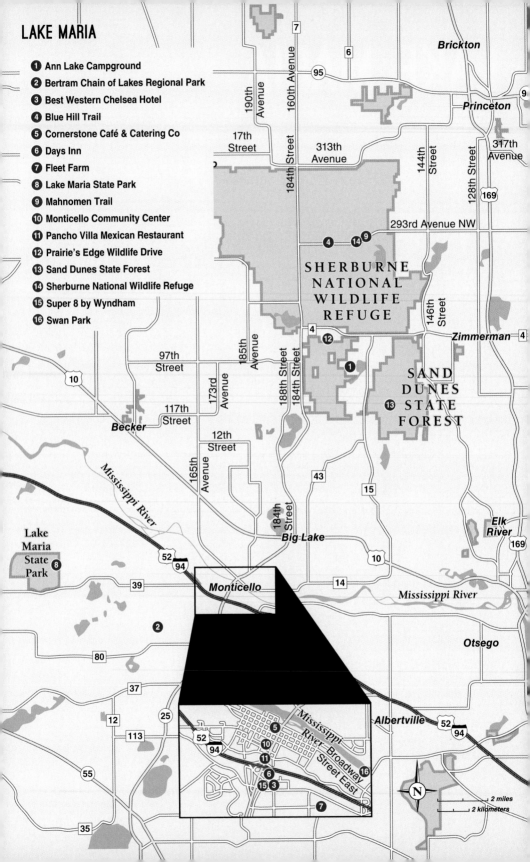

LAKE MARIA

1. Ann Lake Campground
2. Bertram Chain of Lakes Regional Park
3. Best Western Chelsea Hotel
4. Blue Hill Trail
5. Cornerstone Café & Catering Co
6. Days Inn
7. Fleet Farm
8. Lake Maria State Park
9. Mahnomen Trail
10. Monticello Community Center
11. Pancho Villa Mexican Restaurant
12. Prairie's Edge Wildlife Drive
13. Sand Dunes State Forest
14. Sherburne National Wildlife Refuge
15. Super 8 by Wyndham
16. Swan Park

LODGING 🏕

TOP PICK

LAKE MARIA STATE PARK (MINNESOTA DEPARTMENT OF NATURAL RESOURCES) *14111 Clementa Ave. NW, Monticello; 763-878-2325; dnr.state.mn.us /state_parks/park.html?id=spk00217. $13–$19/night for backpack-in sites, 17 sites; $55–$65/night for camper cabins, 3 cabins; reservations required; sites have picnic table, fire ring, grill, food storage boxes, vault toilets near each site, flush toilets in trail center (no showers available). Water is available near trail center or parking lots. State park permit required ($35 annual, $7 daily).*

With all due respect to its 66 counterparts in Minnesota, Lake Maria is what a state park is supposed to look like. It's a reminder of the kind of forest Laura Ingalls Wilder wrote about in *Little House in the Big Woods*—rolling hills covered with old-growth red oak, sugar maple, and basswood trees, which at one time dominated this area of the Midwest. The park is dotted with lakes and ponds and wide, open hiking trails that offer breathtaking views of the canopy, especially during the fall color season.

Lake Maria does have a pair of group camps, but otherwise its campsites are spread across 1,600 acres, making it the

■ Most sites here feel private and secluded.

perfect spot for a quiet camping experience. While a few sites are within shouting distance of each other (including B12 and B13), most are far enough apart that it feels like you're in your own private forest.

The perfect spot if you want the shortest hike is B5, which, like many sites, sits on the edge of a pond. There's a little gravel pad right at the entrance to the trail to the site that you can park on if it's not already occupied (there's only room for two vehicles); from there, it's only a couple hundred yards to the site. But even if there is

■ All sites at Lake Maria have food-storage boxes.

no room there to park, the lot to the west near the group camps is not much farther. B6 also requires only a short walk, but it's tiny and isn't very flat.

Sites B8 and B14 sit above Maria Lake on the southwest side of the park and provide spectacular views (especially of the sunset), but they are among the farthest

■ Lake Maria's camper cabins are a convenient lodging alternative.

sites from parking, each about three quarters of a mile. B4 and B7 are the most remote and are both great sites. B9, B10, B16, and B17 do not sit on water and don't offer much in the way of views, but honestly, it's hard to go very wrong with any of these campsites.

If you're interested in getting out of a car campground but are reticent to hike into a campsite to pitch a tent, Lake Maria offers a nice compromise—the park has three camper cabins. These 12-by-16-foot structures, each sleeping up to six people, allow you to leave the tents and sleeping pads at home and alleviate the concern of getting caught in bad weather away from your vehicle. The camper cabin sites offer the same amenities as the campsites, with a nearby vault toilet, and have woodstoves inside that allow you to use lighter-weight sleeping bags even in cold weather.

The park is a beautiful setting for winter recreation, with more than 6 miles of groomed trails for cross-country skiing and paths for snowshoeing and hiking. Hiking is prohibited on the trails that are groomed in the winter. While all three camper cabins are on ungroomed trails, if you are planning to winter camp in one of the backpacking sites, it's a good idea before making a reservation to check with the park about which sites are accessible.

One of Maria's claims to fame is the presence of the Blanding's turtle, a threatened species that can be seen throughout the park (watch for them on roads and drive carefully). There is a large sculpture of a Blanding's outside the park's trail center.

If you're coming to camp at Lake Maria and need firewood, the park office is generally open only on weekends 11 a.m.–4 p.m. and sporadically during the week. You can't get firewood if the office is closed.

Finally, I would like to note that I'm not trying to give the impression that Lake Maria is only for novice backpackers. It's also a terrific place for experienced trekkers who may not have the time or inclination for a more ambitious trip, but instead are just looking for the kind of therapy that only a night deep in the woods can provide.

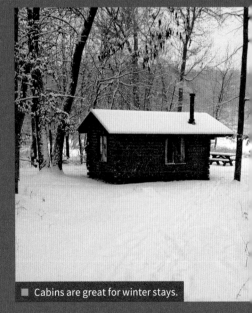
■ Cabins are great for winter stays.

WINTER CAMPING

Granted, winter camping is not for everyone. But many state parks in Minnesota keep their campgrounds open during the winter months, or at least will plow out portions, for people who don't mind sleeping in the cold.

Winter camping does have advantages. No bugs will bother you, and campsite reservations are certainly easier to come by. On the other hand, the days are awfully short, extending the time you might have to spend wrapped up in your sleeping bag. And the joys of summer camping—relaxing in front of a campfire, for example—become a bit more problematic.

But, assuming you winter camp when the temperatures are not drastically low, or you skip going in the middle of a blizzard, tenting in the cold can be an interesting and rewarding experience. Most of your friends may think you're nuts, but that might just be part of the appeal.

A list of which Minnesota parks accommodate winter camping is at dnr.state.mn.us/state_parks/winter_camping_map.html. And you can find more information about programs that will help you learn to winter camp at dnr.state.mn.us/state_parks/winter_camping.html.

BACKUP BASE CAMP

Sand Dunes State Forest, Ann Lake Campground (Minnesota Department of Natural Resources) *Prairie's Edge Wildlife Drive, Big Lake; 763-878-2325 (managed by Lake Maria State Park); dnr.state.mn.us/state_forests/forest.html?id=sft00045. $14/night for drive-in and walk-in sites, 30 drive-in sites, 6 walk-in sites; reservations not available; sites have picnic table, fire ring, grill, vault toilets; water spigots can be found throughout the campground; payment for camping is required via envelope at the entrance to the campground, so bring cash or check.*

During the peak camping season from mid-June to mid-August, Lake Maria's camping occupancy rate is only about 40%, but most of its vacancies occur during the week—it does fill up most weekends. If you can't get a reservation at Maria and want a getaway close to the Twin Cities, Sand Dunes State Forest, which offers traditional drive-in camping in Ann Lake Campground, is a decent alternative. The campsites are relatively close to each other, generally well shielded from the back and sides but open to the road. Because it's a state forest, you can't make reservations for a campsite, but even on busy weekends there are usually a couple of spots open—although to be sure, it's always best to arrive relatively early in the day.

Because the sites are first come, first served, your best bet is to drive through the campground until you find a spot to your liking, unload some gear onto the picnic table, and then return to register at the pay box near the campground entrance.

Sites 9–12 offer the most privacy and as such are usually taken early. Sites 3–8 vary in quality, but they are off the main campground road so have less vehicle traffic. Sites 31–35 are walk-in sites, yet 31 and 34 are so close to parking you can gain some seclusion while still staying within sight of your vehicle. The park does attract both tent campers and people with camping vehicles, but most of the RVs will be in the sites on the main road.

Directions From the Twin Cities, take I-94 west to Rogers and get in the right lane to take Exit 207B to MN 101 N. Follow 101 for 7 miles and take US 10 W toward Elk River. Go 6 miles and take the exit for County Road 15/County Road 14. Turn right on CR 15. In 5.5 miles turn right on 233rd Avenue NW. The park will be 0.8 mile ahead. Watch for the signs for Ann Lake Campground.

INDOOR LODGING

If you need indoor lodging when near Lake Maria, the best options are the basic hotels that have sprung up in the last few years in the newly developed area of Monticello south of I-94.

Super 8 *1114 Cedar St.; 763-219-8649; wyndhamhotels.com/super-8/monticello -minnesota/super-8-monticello-mn/overview; $79–$119/night, free Wi-Fi, free breakfast, indoor pool, queen and king beds*

Days Inn *200 E. Oakwood Drive; 763-295-1111; wyndhamhotels.com/days-inn/monticello -minnesota/days-inn-monticello-mn/overview. $79–$126/night, free Wi-Fi, free breakfast, pet-friendly, queen and king beds, suites*

Best Western Chelsea Hotel *89 Chelsea Road; 763-271-8880, bestwestern.com. $125–$170/night, free Wi-Fi, free breakfast, pet-friendly, queen and king beds, suites*

HIKING

Lake Maria State Park

The longtime manager at Lake Maria, who retired in 2016 after 27 years at the park, took great pride in keeping the park's trails well kept and well signed, and his successor does the same. There are 14 miles of trail in the park, but the various paths intersect so frequently, it's one of the few places you can set out without a planned route and hike for as short or as long as you'd like without fear of getting too far from your car. You can take off right from your campsite, or park near the trail center or the group camps.

■ The big woods in fall color at Lake Maria

The park is hilly, and so are most of the trails, but the elevation changes are relatively moderate and are appropriate for almost everyone. The 3-mile **Anderson Loop Trail** does have a steep portion that leads to an overlook, but it's worth the challenge. You can pick up the Anderson Loop Trail near the equestrian parking lot east of the park's trail center, where it follows the same route as the **Big Woods Loop.** Head north to the overlook, then go west past campsites B1–B3. Turn south and stay on the trail as it heads west, veers south, and then west before reaching the entrance to campsite B6. Go down the hill, cross the park road, and follow the trail until it intersects with the Kettle Kame Trail. Turn left to head back to the trail center.

The 2-mile **Bjorkland Trail** is a nice loop that begins just west of the trail center and winds past Maria Lake (formerly Bjorkland Lake, if your map is old) and past the entrances to several backpack sites.

■ The well-maintained trails at Lake Maria are appropriate for most skill levels.

A quick caution: some trails allow horseback riding, so don't be shocked if you come across an equine or two . . . and, needless to say, you should watch where you step.

If you're looking for a short but educational hike, try the **Zumbrunnen Trail**, a 1-mile trail that goes south from the picnic area east of Little Mary Lake (formerly Maria Lake) at the far western edge of the park. This trail has interpretive signs and observation points.

Sand Dunes State Forest

If you're staying at or visiting Sand Dunes, it offers five loop hikes, none more than a mile long. The easiest is the half-mile **Green Loop** at the north end of the park, but my recommendation if you want a longer trek is to take the **Red Loop** from near the campground entrance, follow it north, and walk up the west side of the **Yellow and Blue Loops.** You'll turn back south just before you reach North Sand Dunes Forest Road, following the east side of the Blue and Yellow Loops until you arrive at the intersection with the Orange Loop. Turn left on the Orange Loop and walk until you get back to the Red Loop, then follow it back to your starting point.

BIKING ⊘

To be honest, this is probably not a trip in which biking should play a central focus. There is a 6-mile bike route in Monticello called the **Broadway Pathway**, alternatively referred to as the **Great River Trail** in connection with its incorporation as part of the **Mississippi River Trail (MRT)**, an effort that links bike trails from northern Minnesota all the way to Louisiana. The Great River trailhead is on the west side of

Monticello near Montissippi Regional Park. The problem is that much of the trail is actually city streets, including through downtown Monticello; it's just not the best choice for a quiet morning ride.

The MRT is a wonderful and welcome idea, but its mix of established bike trails connected by roads and streets can make for difficult and confusing riding, especially for the casual biker. More information on the MRT in Minnesota can be found at dot.state.mn.us/bike/mrt/maps.html.

For mountain bikers, there's a nice collection of singletrack trail totaling about 13 miles at **Bertram Chain of Lakes Regional Park**, just a few minutes from Lake Maria. More information is at mtbproject.com/trail/3505586/bertram-chain-of-lakes.

> ***Directions to Bertram*** The park is about 7 miles from Lake Maria. Turn right outside of the park. In 0.2 mile turn left on CR 39. Go 3.8 miles to Briarwood Avenue NE. Turn right on Briarwood, drive 1.8 miles, and turn left on 90th Street NE. The park entrance will be on the left in about 0.2 mile.

OTHER ADVENTURES ⊕

Sherburne National Wildlife Refuge *17076 293rd Ave. NW, Zimmerman; 763-389-3323; fws.gov/refuge/sherburne*

I first discovered this refuge when looking for sandhill cranes to photograph; the area hosts both resident and migrating birds. But it didn't take long for me to discover how much else the refuge has to offer. If Lake Maria is an overlooked state park, the same can be said for Sherburne, even though it's so close to the Twin Cities.

The centerpiece of the refuge is the 7-mile **Prairie's Edge Wildlife Drive**, a gorgeous oak savannah that is a favorite of birders. You can ask about recent sightings at the refuge headquarters (open weekdays 8 a.m.–4 p.m.) or check fws.gov/refuge/Sherburne/recent_sightings.html. The drive is open to vehicles after the snow has melted in the spring and until winter arrives, but it's closed during the state firearm deer season in November. There are small parking areas adjacent to four wildlife observation decks along the drive and three short hiking trails. Bathroom facilities are just inside the drive entrance.

The refuge also offers year-round access to two scenic hiking trails, **Mahnomen** (3 miles) and **Blue Hill** (5 miles), both located on Sherburne County Road 9. From September 1 to February 28, most of the refuge is open to hiking, with cross-country skiing and snowshoeing as conditions allow. (When the trails are groomed, hikers should walk on the left side of the trail.) The Blue Hill Trail parking lot is a favorite of night-sky photographers, especially those looking for northern lights, because it provides a dark sky and a good view to the north.

Here's a refuge map: fws.gov/uploadedFiles/RefugeMap(2).pdf.

> ***Directions from Lake Maria State Park*** It's about 25 miles to the park office. Turn right out of the park onto Clementa Avenue NW. Turn left on CR 39. In 5.7 miles continue on Golf Course Road, and stay on it as it turns left and becomes Elm Street. In 0.2 mile turn right on W. Broadway Street. In 0.5 mile turn left on MN 25 (Pine Street). In 0.9 mile turn left on CR 17. In 0.5 mile continue on CR 81.

■ Trumpeter swans put on a show at Swan Park.

In 0.7 mile turn right on 206th Avenue and continue straight as it becomes 196th Street. In 0.5 mile turn right on Highline Drive. Continue for 1.2 miles and turn left on 184th Street. In 10 miles turn right on 289th Avenue NW. Go 2 miles to 293rd Avenue NW and continue to the office, on your left.

The Prairie's Edge Wildlife Drive is about 4 miles southwest of the refuge office; you'll pass by it on the way from Lake Maria to the office. But if heading there from the office, go west on 293rd Avenue for 0.2 mile, continue onto 289th Avenue NW for 2 miles, then turn right on 184th Street. In 2 miles, the drive will be on your left.

The Blue Hill Trail is about 0.5 mile west of the refuge office, on the north side of 289th Avenue NW. The Mahnomen Trail is in the opposite direction from the office, about 0.3 mile on 293rd Avenue NW.

Swan Park   *121 Mississippi Drive, Monticello; ci.monticello.mn.us/swanpark*

The park, which sits on the Mississippi River, is open year-round, but it really comes alive in the winter months (November–March, approximately), when it is home to some 2,000 trumpeter swans. Each morning the swans begin to congregate around dawn, waiting for the 1,500 pounds of corn that is fed to them by nearby resident Jim Lawrence. Fencing keeps people from getting too close to the swans, but there are good opportunities to get photographs of the swans feeding and in flight. The best viewing time is from first light until the swans are fed for the first time in the middle of the morning. You can't see the swans (although you can hear them) from the parking area, so you'll be observing them from outside—dress warmly!

Directions   From the Twin Cities, head west on I-94 and take the first Monticello exit, which leads to CR 75 (Broadway Street E). At the first stoplight, turn right on CR 39, drive 0.25 mile, and turn left on Mississippi Drive.

RAINY DAY 😷

If you're at Lake Maria on a rainy day and don't like being tent-bound, a low-key alternative is to hang out at the trail center, which has bathrooms, tables and benches, and a wood-burning stove that is good for taking off a chill.

Otherwise, if you want to head into Monticello:

Monticello Community Center *404 Walnut St., Monticello; 763-295-2954; monticellocommunitycenter.com; open Monday–Thursday 5 a.m.–10 p.m., Friday 5 a.m.–9 p.m., Saturday 7 a.m.–8 p.m., and Sunday 7 a.m. to 4 p.m.; hours for specific activities may vary—check with center for details; admission is $7.75 for adults and $6.75 for those age 17 and under or over 55.*

The community center offers a variety of activities that will keep any kids in your group happy for a few hours, including a swimming pool and waterslide and a play area. There is also a 38-foot-tall climbing wall with a range of difficulty levels.

FOOD AND DRINK 🥤

Cornerstone Café & Catering Co. *154 W. Broadway, Monticello; 763-295-3888; cornerstonecafe.com*

Like many small towns, downtown Monticello has suffered a bit with the commercial development on the edges of the city. But the Cornerstone is a great place in the center of town for a hearty breakfast or any meal. The Hog Pile skillet will give you the calories you need for a long day of adventure; for something a little different, try the creamy chicken wild rice omelet. The almond chicken salad wrap makes a nice lunch.

Pancho Villa Mexican Restaurant *100 W. 7th St., Monticello; 763-314-0454; panchovillasgrill.com*

I feel a little embarrassed that I expected no more than generic chain Mexican fare when I stopped at Pancho Villa. It was a happy surprise that it was much more than that. The burrito dinner got a high grade, as did the torta ahogado, a Mexican sandwich that originated in Guadalajara in the early 1900s. My wife also gave a thumbs-up to the organic margarita.

GEAR AND RESUPPLY 🛒

Fleet Farm *320 Chelsea Rd., Monticello; 763-272-1610; fleetfarm.com*

In an emergency, this is the closest business catering to outdoor needs in Monticello.

The thick forest canopy at Lake Maria shades many of the trails.

The spectacular waterfalls at Minneopa State Park

NEW ULM

One of the fun parts of putting this book together is sharing locations in Minnesota that are off the beaten path. The New Ulm area in south-central Minnesota attracts visitors because of its strong German heritage, but it isn't a locale particularly known for outdoor adventures. That may be because there isn't a spot—like a Grand Marais or a Root River—that serves as a singular recreational draw. However, one state park on the edge of New Ulm and two others a stone's throw away offer a combination of outdoor activities that will more than fill a weekend. In fact, there are outdoor attractions here that are rare anywhere else in Minnesota, and you can get there in less than 2 hours from the Twin Cities.

Areas included: New Ulm, Flandrau State Park, Fort Ridgely State Park, Minneopa State Park, Cottonwood River

Adventures: Camping, biking, hiking, exploring, paddling

Directions: From Bloomington in the Twin Cities, it's about 90 miles to New Ulm via US 169. Take US 169 south about 61 miles and turn right on MN 99 W in St. Peter. Go 12 miles and turn right on US 14. In 2.7 miles turn left on County Road 37 (20th Street S.). In 0.7 mile turn right on S. Valley Street.

NEW ULM

1. August Schell Brewing Company
2. Bingham Hall Bed & Breakfast
3. Cottonwood Grill
4. Deutsche Strasse Bed & Breakfast
5. Flandrau State Park
6. Fort Ridgely
7. Fort Ridgely State Park
8. Hermann Monument
9. Lola American Bistro
10. Minneopa Falls
11. Minneopa State Park
12. Minnesota Music Hall of Fame
13. Nicollet Bike Shop

Winthro

Lafayett

Fort Ridgely
State Park

Old Fort Road

631st Avenue

Minnesota
River

Essig

New
Ulm

Flandrau
State Park

Sleepy Eye

Cottonwood
River

Leavenworth

Searles

Hanska

Godahl

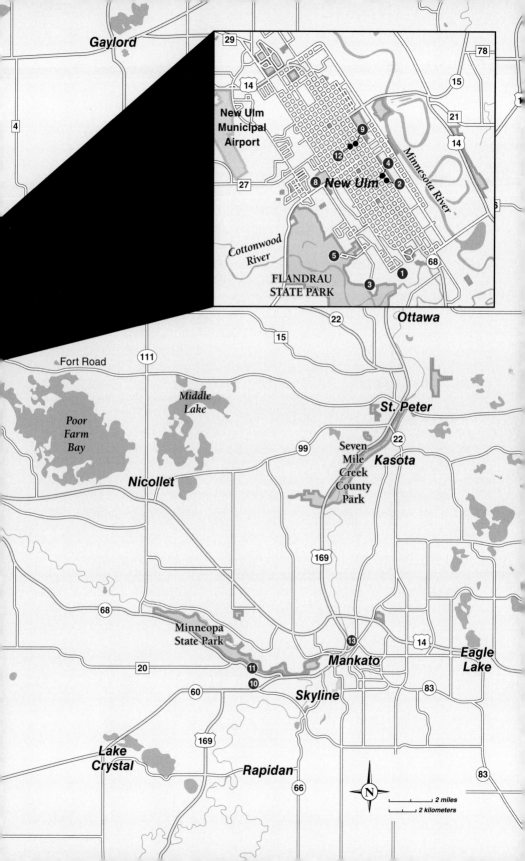

TOP PICK

FLANDRAU STATE PARK (MINNESOTA DEPARTMENT OF NATURAL RESOURCES) *1300 Summit Ave., New Ulm; 507-233-9800; dnr.state.mn.us/state _parks/park.html?id=spk00145. $17–$23/night ($8 more for sites with electric hookups) for drive-in sites in main campground, 48 sites, 16 with electric hookups; $15–$19/night for drive-in sites at rustic campground, 32 sites; reservations required; sites have picnic table, fire ring, grill, flush and vault toilets, water, hot showers and flush toilets May 1–mid-October (check with park for specific dates). Rustic campers should use beach house showers when open. State park permit required ($35 annual, $7 daily).*

The quality of the campsites at Flandrau varies widely. Some are what the park refers to as "nonsecluded," grassy areas with a few trees but not much separating you from your neighbor. Those sites are generally on the inside of the loops or on the outside of loops that butt up against each other. I prefer the rustic campground (no electric hookups), which is more remote than the main "semimodern" campground. If you do end up in the modern campground, the loop with the nonelectric sites is the best option. The rustic campground does not have a shower building, but you can use the one at Flandrau's beach house.

Want to get away from it all? Flandrau has three walk-in campsites near the rustic campground. They offer the most wilderness experience in the park (W91 is the best). You do have to lug your gear from your car to the sites, but it's not far.

If camping at Flandrau, you can enjoy the proximity of the Cottonwood River, or take a dip in the chlorinated, sand-bottom swimming pond, usually open from early June until late August.

Also, because Flandrau was the site of a Works Progress Administration (WPA) camp during the late 1930s and early 1940s, it's fun to take time to check out the buildings in the park that are beautiful examples of the architectural work done by the WPA.

Finally, it's worth noting that Flandrau is right on the edge of New Ulm; you might be surprised when you arrive how close you are to town. So while you're not exactly deep in the wilderness, if you're planning to explore what New Ulm has to offer, it's nice to be so close.

Directions Follow the directions to New Ulm (it's about another 2 miles to the park) but instead of turning on S. Valley Street, stay on 20th Street S and in 0.3 mile turn right on S. Broadway Street. In 0.8 mile turn left on S. 10th Street. In 0.8 mile turn left on Summit Avenue. The park is just ahead to your right.

■ The rustic campground at Flandrau

■ Be sure to check out the bison herd at Minneopa State Park.

BACKUP BASE CAMPS

Minneopa State Park (Minnesota Department of Natural Resources) *54497 Gadwall Road, Mankato; 507-389-5464; dnr.state.mn.us/state_parks/park.html?id=spk00235. $17–$21/night ($8 more for sites with electric hookups) for drive-in sites, 61 sites, 6 with electric hookups; reservations required; sites have picnic table, fire ring, grill, vault toilets, water, hot showers and flush toilets May 1–mid-October (check with park for specific dates); state park permit required ($35 annual, $7 daily).*

Minneopa State Park is about 23 miles southwest of Flandrau, just west of the city of Mankato, and it may be a better choice for camping than Flandrau if you're not interested in doing much exploring in New Ulm. The sites offer more privacy, especially those on the outside of the loops, even though a lot of the sites are open to the road and spaced fairly close together. There is only one campground here, with two loops. Good choices are even-numbered campsites 16–24 in the A loop—they're closest to the Minnesota River—and even-numbered sites 18–34 in the B loop are also good choices.

Minneopa does have two of the coolest things you'll find in any state park in Minnesota—a spectacular set of waterfalls and a unique bison herd.

Minneopa is split into two sections, with the waterfalls across CR 68, south of the campground portion of the park. The falls are a short hike past the shelter in the southern park section. When you park, you can see the shelter. Walk past it, and you'll run into a footbridge with a small set of falls above it. You cross the bridge to follow the path to the large falls. You can stay on the walkway for a nice view of the falls, or follow a steep set of steps (constructed by the WPA) that go to the base of the falls. You'll have to take this route back out—an older trail that looped around the falls has been closed due to erosion. The falls are a popular attraction and can get busy by the middle of the day, so visit in the morning if possible.

Take plenty of time to explore the falls before heading back to the campground side of the park to check out the bison herd, which is maintained at Minneopa as part of an effort between the Minnesota Department of Natural Resources and the Minnesota Zoological Garden to conserve and expand American plains bison with healthy genetics. This kind of herd, largely free of genetic material that can come from cross-breeding with cattle, is rare in Minnesota and the United States.

Mill Road, which can be accessed from near the campground, goes through the 300-acre bison enclosure. You are required to stay in your vehicle. Check with the park to see the best time of day to see the bison gather near the road, which they cross to get to their feeding area; at other times, the bison congregate far from the road and can be difficult to spot. The bison drive is closed on Wednesdays, and open hours vary by season; check with the park office for open hours during your visit.

Like Flandrau, Minneopa has many buildings constructed by the WPA during the 1930s.

> **To reach the falls from the campground** Exit the park, turn left on CR 68, then right on 547th Street (CR 117). Follow the road past the cemetery to Gadwall Road (CR 69). Turn right and go 0.3 mile to the park entrance.

Fort Ridgely State Park (Minnesota Department of Natural Resources) 72158
County Road 30, Fairfax; 507-426-7840; dnr.state.mn.us/state_parks/park.html?id=spk00151. $15–$19/night ($8 more for sites with electric hookups) for drive-in sites, 31 sites, 6 with electric hookups, 3 walk-in sites; reservations required; sites have picnic table, fire ring, grill, vault toilets (flush toilets in the picnic area), water; open April 1–late October (check with park for specific dates); state park permit required ($35 annual, $7 daily).

Fort Ridgely is about 17 miles northwest of New Ulm. When you enter the campgrounds, the small loop to the left has the most spacious sites. The portion of the campground with electric hookups is farther up the road, to the northwest. Some electric sites are close to Fort Ridgely Creek, but they don't offer as much privacy as the sites in the nonelectric loop. There are three walk-in campsites, but be advised that they can only be reached by walking about 300 yards up a steep hill from the parking area.

The main attraction of this park, whether you are camping there or not, is the historic fort site. The fort was built in 1855 and was attacked twice during the US–Dakota War of 1862. A museum on the grounds is operated by the Minnesota Historical Society (separate fee required), but exploring the ruins on the grounds is more fun than the museum. Signs posted around the site explain the fort's history.

Fort Ridgely historical site

You may see an area in the park near the campground that looks something like a golf course, and it was, until 2016. Fort Ridgely was one of the few state parks in Minnesota with its own golf course, but financial losses forced its closure.

INDOOR LODGING

The camper cabins found in many Minnesota state parks are great for people who want to stay overnight in a park but don't have a tent (or aren't interested in sleeping in one). Most of these small cabins provide beds (you'll need to bring a sleeping bag or other bedding), a table and chairs, and a grill and/or fire ring for cooking outside. These are not luxury accommodations by any means, but they can keep you in the midst of the outdoors without the need to set up a campsite or worry about rain. And, occasionally, you get the kind of special cabins available at Flandrau and Fort Ridgely.

Civilian Conservation Corps (CCC) Cabin at Flandrau State Park *1300 Summit Ave., New Ulm; 507-233-9800; dnr.state.mn.us/state _parks/flandrau/cabin.html; $75/night; available mid-May–mid-October (check with park for specific dates).*

CCC cabin at Flandrau State Park

You'll find a number of CCC structures at Flandrau, but this is the only one you can sleep in! The cabin is a former stone kitchen shelter that has been converted to a lodging facility. There's a double bed, with optional trundle. Water can be found near the cabin, with flush toilets and showers available over in the main campground.

Camper Cabins at Flandrau State Park *1300 Summit Ave., New Ulm; 507-233-9800; dnr.state.mn.us/state_parks/reservations_campercabin.html; $60–$70/night; available year-round.*

Flandrau also has two standard camper cabins with electric heat, electricity, and screened porches. They are available year-round, but only Thursdays–Sundays during the winter season. The Coffeetree Retreat Cabin sleeps six and the Hackberry Haven Cabin (ADA accessible) sleeps five.

Farmhouse Cabin at Fort Ridgely State Park *72158 County Road 30, Fairfax; 507-426-7840; dnr.state.mn.us/state_parks/fort_ridgely/farmhouse.html; $70/night; available May 1–late October (check with park for specific dates).*

The farmhouse cabin is located near Fort Ridgely's equestrian campground, which is separate from the main park. The farmhouse has three beds, including a set of bunk beds, and will sleep up to six people. A small refrigerator is provided, and the house has air-conditioning but no heat. Meals need to be cooked outside, on the grill or fire ring. A vault toilet is located near the farmhouse, and you can use the flush toilets and showers in the equestrian campground.

Chalet Cabin at Fort Ridgely State Park *72158 County Road 30, Fairfax; 507-426-7840; dnr.state.mn.us/state_parks/fort_ridgely/chalet.html; $60–$80/night; available year-round.*

This cabin has a full kitchen with utensils. There is a fireplace and central heat but no beds—you'll have to roll out your sleeping bag on the floor. Bathrooms are on the lower level.

Camper Cabin at Minneopa State Park *54497 Gadwall Road, Mankato; 507-389-5464; dnr.state.mn.us/state_parks/reservations_campercabin.html; $60–$70/night; available year-round.*

Minneopa has one standard camper cabin with electricity, propane heat, a woodstove, and a porch. It is available year-round, but only Thursdays–Sundays during the winter season, and sleeps five.

If you're looking for something besides a state park cabin, here are a couple of options:

Deutsche Strasse Bed & Breakfast *404 S. German St., New Ulm; 507-354-2005; deutschestrasse.com; $119–$199/night*

Most chain hotels offer a free breakfast, which, as you've probably found, is often one step above cardboard. The morning meal is definitely not an afterthought at the Deutsche Strasse, a home built in 1884 and converted to a B&B in 1997. The four-course breakfast will get you ready for whatever outdoor adventure you have planned for the day. Five rooms are available, all with private baths. Fireplaces can be found in all but the Flower room, with whirlpools in the Crystal room and Black Forest Suite. The latter is a good choice if you need a bit more room.

Bingham Hall Bed & Breakfast *505 S. German St. New Ulm; 507-276-5070; bingham-hall.com; $109–$199/night*

Your best choice here is either the Elijah or the Henle, both elegant period rooms, with fireplaces and whirlpool baths. The McKeeth (whirlpool but no fireplace) and Lothards (no fireplace or whirlpool) rooms are a bit more traditional, so not as much fun.

HIKING ⊙

Flandrau State Park *About 3 miles*

Starting from the south parking lot, across from the visitor center next to the Cottonwood River, walk southeast past the volleyball courts to the **River Trail.** You'll get to a river overlook and a steep set of steps. Follow the River Trail 0.3 mile up the bluff and then take one side of the loop or the other—either the **Old Island Loop Trail** (0.6 mile) or the **Old Dam Trail** (0.4 mile). Both will take you to the River Loop Trail, which is about a mile from where the trail ends at the site of a former dam. Return either the way you came, or take the other side of the loop.

The dam was built in the early 1940s by the CCC, creating a 200-acre reservoir on the river. The dam was damaged by high water numerous times and was finally removed in 1995.

■ Make time to visit the waterfalls at Minneopa State Park.

Minneopa State Park *About 4.5 miles*

The bison enclosure is in the middle of this hiking trail, but don't worry—the big animals are fenced in! From the southwest edge of the campground, follow the **Minnesota River Bluff Trail** counterclockwise about 3.1 miles to the intersection with the **Seppmann Mill Trail.** From there, it's about 1.3 miles back to the campground.

While you're at the intersection, you can take a spur trail to the windmill, where you'll also find a scenic overlook. The main portion of the windmill, which was completed in 1864, still stands, but the arms were damaged and not rebuilt after a tornado hit the structure in 1890.

If you want to see the windmill without taking the hike, there is parking a short distance from the beginning of the spur trail.

BIKING @

While there are limited biking opportunities in the state parks covered in this chapter, the city of New Ulm has designated a 13-mile bike loop around the city, a paved recreation trail clearly marked with arrows painted on the streets. Benches and bike racks can be found along the route. The city of New Ulm has a map of the route at newulm.com/wp-content/uploads/2017/11/New_Ulm_Biking_Route_Maps_Oct_2017.pdf. Information can also be found at heartsbeatback.org/Bike%20New%20Ulm. In addition, you can pick up a map at the New Ulm Visitor Center (1 North Minnesota Street).

While the **Sakatah Singing Hills State Trail** is a bit outside the parameters of this chapter, about 28 miles from New Ulm (just north of Mankato), it is a wonderful trail and the closest dedicated longer trail to New Ulm. The 39-mile path, built on a former rail bed, begins at Lime Valley Road near US 14. It meets up with the Minnesota River Trail in Mankato, proceeds through Waterville, and then hits Sakatah Lake State Park before ending just east of I-35 in Faribault. While the trail is long, it is generally flat. It's easy to pick out a distance and turn around at your halfway point. A map is available at files.dnr.state.mn.us/maps/state_trails/sakatah.pdf.

PADDLING ⊗

The **Cottonwood River** has good paddling for about 60 miles before it meets the Minnesota River at New Ulm, but it only offers scenic paddling—woods on both sides of the water, instead of farmland—for about the last 20 miles. There are a number of good spots to put in above New Ulm, as shown on the map that can be found at files. dnr.state.mn.us/maps/canoe_routes/minnesota3.pdf.

RAINY DAY 😎

August Schell Brewing Company   *1860 Schell Road, New Ulm; 507-354-5528; schellsbrewery.com*

Schell is a Minnesota tradition, even in this era of craft beers. Tours of the brewery are offered Friday–Sunday, with tickets available at the Museum of Brewing, which opens one hour before the first tour (11 a.m. on Saturday and noon on Friday and Sunday). Tickets are $5 and are first come, first served; tours do occasionally sell out, so it's best to get there early.

Schell's Starkeller brewing facility and taproom (507-359-7827) is located about 4 miles from the main brewery grounds, at 2215 North Garden Street in New Ulm. The Starkeller, open Fridays 4–9 p.m. and Saturdays 2–9 p.m., features the brewer's line of sour Berliner Weiss–style beers.

Hermann Monument   *10 Monument St., New Ulm; hermannmonument.com; open Memorial Day–Labor Day, daily, 10 a.m.– 7 p.m.; Saturdays and Sundays in May and September; and Fridays, Saturdays, and Sundays the first three weekends in October; $3 per person, children ages 5 and under admitted free with a paying adult; for safety reasons, all youth ages 15 and under must be accompanied by an adult.*

Hermann the German, as the locals call it, has towered over New Ulm since 1897. The statue depicts Hermann the Cheruscan and commemorates Germania's victory over the Romans at the Battle of the Teutoburg Forest, a symbol of German patriotism. Visitors to the statue can climb the spiral staircase to an observation platform at the base of the statue, which commands a view of the town and the Minnesota River Valley below.

Minnesota Music Hall of Fame *27 N. Broadway, New Ulm; 507-354-7305; mnmusichalloffame.org; open Thursday–Saturday, 10 a.m.–2 p.m.; admission, $5*

New Ulm was proposed as the site of the Minnesota Music Hall of Fame in 1962, with the goal of honoring musicians who have made significant contributions to music in Minnesota. But it took a few years to get the project moving, with the hall of fame museum opening in 1987. There are some 155 inductees featured, including Judy Garland, Bob Dylan, and Prince.

FOOD AND DRINK 🍴

Cottonwood Grill *1 Golf Drive, New Ulm; 507-354-8896, golfnewulm.com/cottonwood-grill*

The Cottonwood Grill is at the New Ulm Country Club, but this is Minnesota, folks— you don't have to worry about being fancy. The food is nothing fancy either—burgers, sandwiches, salads—but meals are nicely done in a pleasant atmosphere.

Lola American Bistro *16 N. Minnesota St., New Ulm; 507-359-2500; lolaamericanbistro.com*

If it happens to be raining and you don't want to make breakfast at the campsite, Lola has a good selection of hearty morning fare—and they have espresso! If you swing by for lunch or dinner, try the pot pies or glazed salmon.

GEAR AND RESUPPLY 🛒

Nicollet Bike Shop *607 N. Riverfront Drive, Mankato; 507-388-9390; nicolletbike.com*

The only honest-to-goodness bike shop we found anywhere close to New Ulm is this one, about a half hour southeast in Mankato but only a few minutes east of Minneopa State Park.

The headwaters of the Mississippi is a must-see attraction at Itasca State Park.

NORTHWEST

When my kids were young, we managed to visit every state park in Minnesota—with the exception of a half dozen in the northwest corner of the state. We had traveled throughout Minnesota over a number of years from the Twin Cities, but the northwest seemed so distant, we just never made it up there. That was a mistake, I realized some years later when I finally spent time in the region and found the parks scenic, distinctive, and—as a bonus—almost empty even on many weekends. With the help of this book, you can avoid the mistake I made.

But to do that, this chapter has to break our "rule" that all of a weekend's activities be within a half hour or so of our main campground. Here, you're going to move campgrounds, and there's a lot of driving between as you visit these six parks . . . or five, if you take a slightly abbreviated trip.

It might be an ambitious task for those of you from the Twin Cities area, but I've done it, and with a little planning you can too. If you're closer to the northwest than the Twin Cities, it'll be that much easier; if you're farther, it's going to take more than a weekend (another rule we'll break, just for this chapter).

There is some method to this madness. A big goal of this chapter is to help out those of you who may be participating in the state park Hiking Club, or considering it (see page 101 for details). While being part of the club does not require you to hike in every state park, it does reward hitting them all, and many people in the club have that as their ultimate goal. So here's an opportunity to knock off six parks in a few days—if that's not an adventure weekend, I don't know what is.

Areas included: Hayes Lake State Park, Old Mill State Park, Lake Bronson State Park, Zippel Bay State Park, Lake Bemidji State Park, Itasca State Park, Mississippi River headwaters

Adventures: Camping, hiking, biking, exploring

THE HIKING CLUB

One of the interesting things about kids is that they have enough energy to race around a playground or ball field all day long, but when it comes to physical activity that they perceive as work, all of a sudden they are dead tired—and often not at all reticent to let you know they *can't take even one more single step.*

That's where the brilliance of the Hiking Club, operated by Minnesota state parks, comes in. Each state park has a Hiking Club trail marked as such at the trailhead. Somewhere on each trail is a sign with a Hiking Club password. Club members need to find the sign with the word and write it down in their club book. With my kids, hiking all of a sudden became a game. Where is the sign? Can we guess what the password might be? On the Hiking Club trails, there was no fatigue . . . and no whining. (By the way, adults can join the club too.)

To make it even better, club members earn a patch when they reach certain mileage milestones, and a plaque if they hike all the trails. There are also free nights of camping to be had, which makes parents especially happy.

The trails with the passwords range in length from 1 mile to 6.2 miles. Sometimes the sign is within a very short distance from the trailhead, but most are pretty close to the halfway point.

(As an aside, please avoid doing what I did. During a winter trek on a Hiking Club trail, my son's record book fell out of my pocket. When I couldn't find it upon returning to our car, I retraced my steps, and fortunately spotted it in the middle of the trail, about a mile out. I nearly lost about five years of hiking records! After that, we carried with us a copy of the book, not the original.)

Hiking Club kits cost $14.95 and can be purchased at most state parks, by calling 651-259-5600, or stopping by the Department of Natural Resources Information Center (500 Lafayette Road, Saint Paul).

The parks also operate a Passport Club, which rewards you for just visiting parks. If you're hitting them anyway, it's worth consideration. Information on both clubs can be found at dnr.state.mn.us/state_parks/clubs.

LODGING AND LOGISTICS

To do this weekend, you'll need two of the six parks for lodging. The first one will be either **Zippel Bay State Park** or **Hayes Lake State Park**, depending on which of the two of our itineraries you choose. **Itasca State Park** will be home for your second night. For the purposes of this itinerary, I will assume you're leaving from the Twin Cities (and apologies to those of you in other parts of the state).

The **first itinerary** will take you on Day One to **Old Mill State Park**, on to **Lake Bronson State Park**, then to Zippel for camping. The total trip is about 12 hours, which includes time to complete the Hiking Club trails at Old Mill and Bronson. The next morning, you'll walk the Hiking Club trail at Zippel, then drive to Hayes Lake State Park, go on to **Lake Bemidji State Park**, and finally to Itasca. If you're out of Zippel by 10 a.m., you'll have time to do the trails at Hayes and Bemidji and arrive at Itasca by late afternoon or early evening.

The **second itinerary** skips Zippel, allowing you to camp at Hayes Lake. This only cuts about an hour from the first day's itinerary, but Hayes Lake is my favorite campground in this part of the state. With this itinerary, on Day One you'll head to Old Mill State Park, then to Lake Bronson State Park, and on to Hayes Lake. You should have time to complete the Hiking Club trails at Old Mill and Bronson and arrive at Hayes Lake by midevening. The next morning, you'll walk the Hiking Club trail at Hayes Lake, then drive to Lake Bemidji State Park, walk the trail, and then head to Itasca. If you're out of Hayes Lake by 10 a.m., you'll have time to do the trail at Bemidji and arrive at Itasca by midafternoon.

With either itinerary, you can complete the Hiking Club trail at Itasca either upon arrival or the following morning before heading home.

Note: You may notice there is another state park in this general vicinity, Franz Jevne, which is about an hour east of Zippel Bay. There was really no way to include it in this trek and still give you time to sleep. If you need it for the Hiking Club, I'd visit it on a different trip, maybe one to the north-central part of the state, along with Scenic, McCarthy Beach, and Lake Vermilion–Soudan Underground Mine State Parks.

Directions from Twin Cities to Old Mill State Park

This drive is about 5.5 hours from the Twin Cities. Leave the cities on I-94, and once you've hit Rogers, continue on I-94 for about 185 miles. Take Exit 22 to MN 9 and follow it about 76 miles to US 2 in Fairfax Township. Turn left on US 2 toward Crookston and then take US 75 north 45 miles until you reach E. Johnson Avenue in Warren. Turn

right, then turn left on N. 2nd Street (US 75). Go 0.4 mile and turn right on County Road 3/ Great Eastern. In about 10 miles continue on 240th Avenue NW. Go about 2 miles, and turn left on CR 128. The park will be on your left about 0.5 mile ahead.

Directions from Old Mill State Park to Lake Bronson State Park

About 31 miles. Turn right out of the park, go south on 240th Avenue NW, and turn left on 320th Street NW. Go 3 miles and turn right on 27th Avenue NW. Follow the road about 14 miles. About 2 miles after it turns into CR 20, turn right on MN 11. Go 1 mile and turn left on CR 20. Drive 6 miles and turn right on Cleveland Avenue in Halma. In 0.2 mile turn left on US 59. Go 4.6 miles and turn right on CR 10. In 1 mile turn left on CR 28, and in another mile, turn left to stay on 28. The park will be on your right about 0.7 mile ahead.

Directions from Lake Bronson State Park to Zippel Bay State Park

About 92 miles. Take CR 28 out of the park and turn right at 375th Avenue to go south on 28. In 1 mile turn left on CR 10. Go about 12 miles and continue on 210th Street for 10 miles. Just past Greenbush, turn left on MN 11 and drive 55 miles. Turn left on CR 140, and in about 5 miles continue onto CR 8 NW. In about 12 miles turn left on 54th Avenue NW and drive about a mile to the park, which will be on your right.

Directions from Lake Bronson State Park to Hayes Lake State Park About 56 miles. Follow CR 28 to CR 10, about 1.7 miles. Turn left on CR 10 and drive about 12 miles. Continue onto 210th Street and drive 20 miles. Continue onto CR 4/300th Avenue and go 11.6 miles to MN 89 S. Turn right, and in 2 miles, turn left on CR 4. In 8.7 miles turn right onto River Forest Road. The park will be on your right.

■ Rustic signage at Hayes Lake

Directions from Zippel Bay State Park to Hayes Lake State Park About 45 miles. Head south on 54th Avenue NW. Turn right on CR 8 and travel about 12 miles; continue onto CR 140 for 5 miles. Turn right on MN 11. In 1.2 miles turn left on CR 2 and continue on 640th Avenue for 0.8 mile. In 2 miles continue on CR 12. In 3 miles turn left on 590th Avenue, drive 6.7 miles, and turn right on Thompson Forest Road. Drive 12.4 miles and turn left on River Forest Road. The park is on the right.

Directions from Hayes Lake State Park to Lake Bemidji State Park About 125 miles. Head northwest on River Forest Road toward CR 4. Turn left on CR 4 and drive 2.7 miles to CR 9. Take a left on CR 9 and drive 7 miles. Continue onto Marshall 54 NW for 11.3 miles and 400th Street for about 5 miles. Just past Grygla, turn left on MN 89 and drive 54 miles, then turn right to stay on 89. In about 20 miles turn left on Grange Road NW. In 6 miles turn right on Irvine Avenue NW. In 2 miles turn left on Town Hall Road NW. In 0.6 mile continue onto Glidden Road NE for 0.8 mile. Turn left on Bemidji Road NE/US 71 Old. In 0.3 mile turn right on Birchmont Beach Road NE. In 1.5 miles turn right on State Park Road NE. The park is 0.6 mile ahead on the right.

Directions from Lake Bemidji State Park to Itasca State Park About 40 miles. Go west on State Park Road NE toward Birchmont Beach Road NW. In 0.6 mile turn left on Birchmont Beach Road NW and drive 1.5 miles. Turn left on Bemidji Road NE/US 71 Old and go about 5 miles. Continue onto Paul Bunyan Drive SE/US 2 Old for 1.2 miles and continue on Washington Avenue SE for 3.3 miles. Follow US 71 S for 12.3 miles and turn right to stay on 71. Go 13.8 miles and turn right on MN 200 W. In 0.2 mile turn left on CR 123/48. In 1.2 miles turn left at CR 122/1 to enter the park.

Directions from Itasca State Park to Twin Cities About 185 miles. This is not a cop-out. There are numerous routes from Itasca to the Twin Cities, so we'll just give highlights here. One way is to take MN 71 south from the park to MN 87, then south on MN 6 and 23 until going east on MN 10 to Motley. I prefer heading east from the park on MN 71/200 and turning south on MN 64 to Motley. Either way, you can then take US 10 to I-94, either cutting over at Clear Lake to Clearwater, or going on to Monticello. Then head on in to the Twin Cities.

TOP PICKS

HAYES LAKE STATE PARK (MINNESOTA DEPARTMENT OF NATURAL RESOURCES)

48990 County Road 4, Roseau; 218-425-7504; dnr.state.mn.us/state_parks/park .html?id=spk00174. $15/night for drive-in sites, 35 sites, 18 with electric hookups; $55–$70/night for camper cabins, 2 cabins, open April 1–October, no heat, Timberline cabin has electricity; $15/night for walk-in sites, 2 sites; reservations required; sites have picnic table, fire ring, grill, showers, flush and vault toilets; state park permit required ($35 annual, $7 daily).

Hayes Lake is a pretty park, with plenty of hiking along the lake and a nice swimming beach and picnic area, the nicest amenities of the parks you'll encounter in the early part of your excursion. The campground is basic, without much privacy (especially in Loop A). Sites 1–11 and 21–26 are in the same cluster and don't have electric hookups, so you're more likely to have tent campers in those spots. That said, this is going to be the only park where I recommend you try to get one specific site for sleeping—and in this case, it's a camper cabin, not a camp-

■ This camper cabin occupies a prime spot at Hayes Lake.

site. It is the best-placed camper cabin I've seen in any state park, located down a long dirt road that opens up into a meadow about the size of a football field, the cabin sitting off by itself right on the edge of the lake. There is no occasion for anyone else to come anywhere near—there's nothing else down the road—so it's like your own private property for the night.

The cabin has a picnic table and fire ring/grill with a vault toilet nearby, but there's no need to bring sleeping pads (there are four beds in the cabin) or a tent. Food, drinks, and sleeping bags should cover it, but because there is no electricity in the cabin, bring a portable charger if you need to rejuice a smartphone. Besides the beauty and privacy of the setting, staying in a camper cabin gives you a little less work on this busy trip—you'll save time by not needing to set up or take down a tent.

To get to the cabin, pass the campground turnoff after entering the park, head west on the park road, and then follow it south. You'll turn at the road with a sign for the Camp 3 cabin—there are only two cabins, so I'm not sure why the designation, but that's what the sign reads.

ITASCA STATE PARK (MINNESOTA DEPARTMENT OF NATURAL RESOURCES)

*36750 Main Park Drive, Park Rapids; 218-699-7251; dnr.state.mn.us/state_parks
/park.html?id=spk00181. $17–$23/night for drive-in sites, 223 sites in two campgrounds,
160 with electric hookups; $17–$23/night for cart-in sites, 11 sites; $13–$19/night for
backpack sites, 11 sites; extensive lodging options, including lodge rooms, cabins,
guesthouse, and group center; reservations required; sites have picnic table, fire ring,
grill, showers, flush and vault toilets; state park permit required ($35 annual, $7 daily).*

What can you say about Itasca? It's kind of like a city unto itself. The first state
park in Minnesota, it's one of the biggest and most popular, and you could easily
spend a week here. Everything about Itasca seems oversize—32,000 acres and more
than 100 lakes within its borders, just for starters. It has three major entrances,
a massive visitor center, restaurants, two
huge campgrounds, nearly 50 miles of
hiking trails, and 16 miles of bike paths.
That's just a start, and I'm already out
of breath. But the biggest attraction, the
place everyone in Minnesota has to visit
at one time or another, is the headwaters
of the Mississippi River, the spot where
the river begins its 2,500-mile journey to
the Gulf of Mexico.

■ Check out the displays at the
Mississippi Headwaters Center.

From the park's north entrance, the
Mary Gibbs Mississippi Headwaters Center
is only a short drive, and from the parking
lot it's only a minute's walk to the headwaters. On summer weekends, the place
is jammed with people having their photo
taken as they step across the river. (Yes,
you gotta do it.) Weekdays are usually not
as crowded, and it's not bad at all before
Memorial Day and after Labor Day.

Despite all of that, the camping at Itasca is largely pedestrian. Sites 1–81 are
in the Bear Paw Campground, and all are electric except 2, 5, 6, 8, 9, 10, 12, and 14,
which are on the outside of the loop. There are cart-in sites north of them that provide
more privacy for a little bit of work. I prefer the Pine Ridge Campground, but I would
try to stay away from the Oak and Spruce Loops, where the quarters can be tight. The
Maple Loop is a bit better. All sites in those three loops are electric. The best camping
I've found at Itasca is on the Pine and Poplar Loops in the Pine Ridge Campground;
the sites are a little roomier, especially on the outside of the loops, and lack electric
hookups, so they're aimed more at tent campers.

This adventure weekend is not the time to try to see everything at Itasca, of
course, but you should have enough time to visit the headwaters and take a look
around the park. It should give you a sense of what the place has to offer, and you can
spend more time exploring during later visits.

ZIPPEL BAY STATE PARK (MINNESOTA DEPARTMENT OF NATURAL RESOURCES)

3684 54th Ave. NW, Williams; 218-783-6252; dnr.state.mn.us/state_parks/park .html?id=spk00284. $15–$19/night for drive-in sites, 57 sites, none with electric hookups; reservations required; sites have picnic table, fire ring, grill, showers, flush and vault toilets; camping available from late April to late October, with water and showers from early May until early October (check with the park for specific dates); state park permit required ($35 annual, $7 daily).

Zippel Bay is the northernmost park in the Minnesota system (Garden Island is farther north, but it's a state recreation area), and it's about as different from Itasca as you can get. It has four very small campgrounds, none with more than 16 sites, and about 6 miles of hiking trails. The park sits on the massive Lake of the Woods, which offers spectacular views, as well as swimming, fishing, and 2 miles of sandy shoreline.

Sites in the campgrounds are generally tightly spaced, and getting one with much privacy is hit and miss. I prefer sites 1, 5, or 6 in the Lady's Slipper Campground, or sites 28, 29, 35, or 36 in the Ridge Campground. Sites in the Angler's Campground (42–57) are a bit larger and better spaced than in some of the others.

One of the more spacious campsites at Zippel Bay

INDOOR LODGING

If you need indoor lodging in an emergency on your first night of this trip, the options are limited except when you are near Roseau, Warroad, or, a little off your path, Baudette. For your second night, you can check out the numerous lodging options at Itasca at dnr.state.mn.us/state_parks/itasca/lodging.

HIKING

Below are the trails with the Hiking Club passwords.

Old Mill State Park *1.4 miles*

When you enter the park, pass the park office and go straight, until you run into the parking area. The Agassiz Trail starts southwest of the parking lot and traverses most of the southern portion of the park, in a loop. At roughly the halfway mark, there is an overlook with views of the Middle River.

Lake Bronson State Park *3.4 miles*

Enter the park at its northwest corner, from CR 28, about a mile east of Lake Bronson. Follow the park road southeast to the parking lot for the picnic area, beach, and volleyball courts. Take the trail north

■ The settlers cabin at Old Mill State Park provides a look at early pioneer life.

from the parking area. It will shortly head northeast and then east before beginning a loop that follows the contour of the campground. The trail meanders along Lake Bronson before going straight north, then west, then southwest. You'll take a spur trail west, and then head back to your car.

Zippel Bay State Park *1.5 miles*

The trails are not named at Zippel Bay, but when you enter the park, traveling north on CR 34/54th Avenue NW, you will see the park office. Go straight, past the turn for the campgrounds, to near the beach and the picnic area at the edge of Lake of the Woods. Starting at the northwest corner of Big Beach, you'll follow the trail northwest up the shore, until you get to the Zippel Bay channel. Turn around and return on the same path.

Hayes Lake State Park *2 miles*

You can find the beginning of the Pine Ridge Trail near the campground, at the south end of Loop A. Hike west and then north, following the shore of the lake. Hike onto the dam, then back to the car via the dam entrance road and campground entrance road.

Lake Bemidji State Park *2.5 miles*

The trail through a spruce/tamarack bog starts on the far north end of the campground, but don't park by the camper cabins—park in the Aspen Lane Campground parking area. You'll see an exhibit panel there about the bog, with information and a map. The trail heads north, crosses CR 20, and then turns east. You'll turn right at the intersection near the vault toilet. Soon you'll see another panel describing the bog, and also a rack where bicyclists can lock their bikes (which cannot go on the raised bogwalk). Continue to the raised bogwalk, which is about a quarter mile long and allows you to hike easily through this boggy area. Return to your starting point by going back on the same trail.

Itasca State Park *3.5 miles*

The best way to enter the park (and there are many) and be close to the Hiking Club trail is to use the east entrance from US 71 and follow the East Entrance Road west to the Historic Douglas Lodge parking area. You will start your hike near the large kiosk. Head south on the Ozawindib Trail, cross Wilderness Drive, and pass Mary Lake to your east. Take the Crossover Trail west to Myrtle Lake, where you will turn north on Deer Park Trail. The trail will again cross Wilderness Drive. When it intersects the Dr. Roberts Trail, turn east. The route ends below the clubhouse, behind the lodge.

FOOD AND DRINK 🍳

We're breaking the rules here again! Given the amount of time you're going to be on the road on this trip, it's tough to figure where you might be at meal time—and to save time, in any case, I'd suggest this is a good trip to pack lunches and enjoy preparing breakfast and dinner at your campsite. There are restaurants and grocery outlets at Itasca that you can visit should you choose.

GEAR AND RESUPPLY 🛒

The limitations you run into for indoor lodging on this route also apply to gear and resupply, although you do drive through numerous small towns in which you can find convenience stores, gas stations, and grocery stores. The best bet near Itasca is **Rock Creek General Store** (218-266-3996, rockcreekgeneralstore.com) near the north entrance to the park at 16879 North Entrance, Park Rapids.

Dock at Hayes Lake

View from the trail at Blue Mounds State Park

ROCK COUNTY

Minnesota, as everybody knows, is the Land of 10,000 Lakes. So it's not surprising that many of the state's recreational activities revolve around water. But I would make the argument that Minnesota has topography as diverse as almost anywhere in the country, allowing for plenty of outdoor adventures that have little or nothing to do with water.

Let's take Rock County as an example. Located in the far southwest corner of the state, Rock County features miles of stunning prairie landscape that is getting harder and harder to find anywhere, let alone in Minnesota. And as much as I love the big woods and water of Minnesota, the prairie has a unique beauty and evokes a bygone era. (Laura Ingalls Wilder, anyone?)

What makes this area of Minnesota special, however, is an additional bit of terrain responsible for the establishment of Blue Mounds State Park, which sits at the center of the county. The park takes its name from a wall of Sioux quartzite that rises nearly 100 feet high and runs 1.5 miles along the edge of the park. The moniker comes from settlers who saw the colored rock as they traveled west in the 1860s. The park's 1,500 acres of prairie allow you to walk through the grasslands atop the cliffs, where you can see for miles in any direction, or to hike or bike along trails at the base of the rocks, where you can appreciate the immensity of the formation.

For trivia buffs, Rock County is one of only four counties in Minnesota without a single lake, but that's OK. Here, your adventure weekend doesn't require water.

Areas included: Blue Mounds State Park, Luverne, Blue Mounds and Casey Jones Trails

Adventures: Camping, biking, hiking, exploring, rock climbing

Directions: To get to Blue Mounds State Park from the Twin Cities, take MN 169 south about 100 miles to MN 60, southwest of Mankato. Follow MN 60 about 90 miles to Worthington. Go west on I-90 about 30 miles to Luverne. Go north on US 75 about 6 miles to the park.

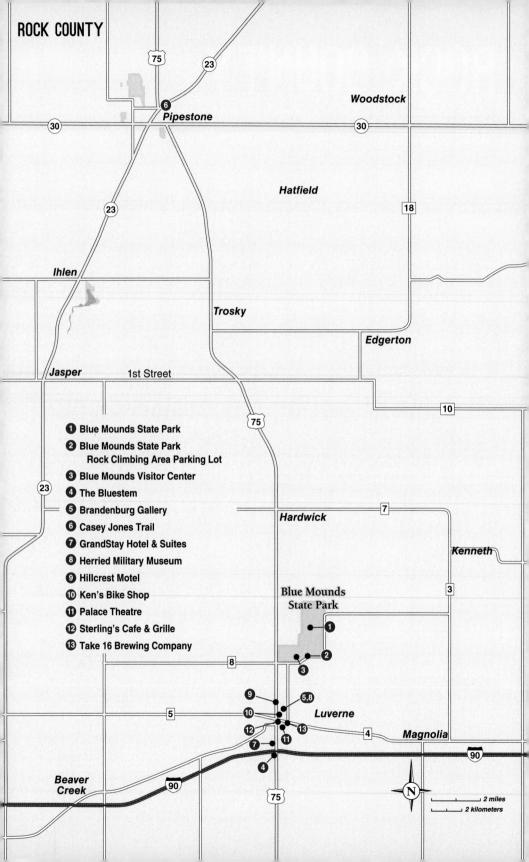

ROCK COUNTY

75
23
Woodstock
6 Pipestone
30   30
18

Hatfield

23

Ihlen

Trosky

Edgerton

Jasper   1st Street

75   10

❶ Blue Mounds State Park
❷ Blue Mounds State Park
    Rock Climbing Area Parking Lot
❸ Blue Mounds Visitor Center   Hardwick   7
❹ The Bluestem
❺ Brandenburg Gallery   Kenneth
❻ Casey Jones Trail
❼ GrandStay Hotel & Suites
❽ Herried Military Museum
❾ Hillcrest Motel   3
❿ Ken's Bike Shop   Blue Mounds
⓫ Palace Theatre   State Park
⓬ Sterling's Cafe & Grille   ❶
⓭ Take 16 Brewing Company
23
                                                              ❷
                                            ❸
                                    8
                                        ❾   ❺,❽
                                    5   ❿   Luverne
                                        ⓬   ⓭   4   Magnolia
                                        ❼ ⓫
                                        ❹
Beaver   90
Creek   90
                    75   N
                                                                    2 miles
                                                                    2 kilometers

LODGING

TOP PICK

BLUE MOUNDS STATE PARK (MINNESOTA DEPARTMENT OF NATURAL RESOURCES) *1410 161st St., Luverne; 507-283-6050; dnr.state.mn.us/state_parks /park.html?id=spk00121. $17–$21/night ($25–$29/night for sites with electric hookup) for drive-in campground, 73 sites, 40 with electric hookups; $13–$19/night for walk- or cart-in sites, 14 sites; $30/night for tepees, available mid-May–mid-September (check with park for specific dates), reservations required; sites have picnic table, fire ring, grill, flush and vault toilets, water, and hot showers (available seasonally—check with park for specific dates). Only a limited number of campsites are available from late fall until early spring. State park permit required ($35 annual, $7 daily).*

Blue Mounds State Park is about 215 miles from the Twin Cities. The drive-in campground here is fine, with most sites shaded by trees to the rear but relatively open to the road in the front. The cart-in sites are better for both privacy and aesthetics, requiring only a short walk (100–300 feet). Cart-in sites 3, 12, and 14 are the most private, but 13 or 14 will put you closest to the bathroom; the only showers are in the drive-in campground.

All that said, if you have the chance to snag one of the three tepees located on the southeast end of the cart-in campground, do not hesitate. Blue Mounds is one of only two state parks in Minnesota (Upper Sioux Agency is the other) that has tepees. Each canvas structure is 18 feet in diameter with a cedar deck for a floor and offers the same amenities as a regular campsite (fire ring with grill and picnic table). The tepees are said to sleep six, which could certainly be done, but you'll be at close quarters—I'd say

four people would be comfortable. Instructions inside each tepee tell you how to adjust the top to provide ventilation (open) or keep dry in case of rain (closed), but I'm not sure I'd want to be outside fiddling with the flaps at 3 a.m. in the middle of a thunderstorm. Fortunately, there's also a "tepee within a tepee" that can be unfurled from inside to provide cover for most but not all of the floor without you having to go out into the elements. The door to the tepee also has a flap that can be rolled over it to provide privacy or to help keep out mosquitoes.

My only complaint about the tepees—a minor one—is that they are a little closer together than I think is ideal. Still, it's a small price to pay for a unique camping experience.

BACKUP BASE CAMPS

If you're tenting, there aren't really any alternatives to Blue Mounds that I can whole-heartedly recommend in the area. Magnolia (about 9 miles east of Luverne) and Adrian (about 14 miles east) have municipal campgrounds, but neither is a place where you would be thrilled to pitch a tent. That said, you shouldn't have any problem getting a reservation at Blue Mounds; only about a third of the park's campsites are occupied during peak season, from mid-June to mid-August. Occupancy will be higher on weekends, of course, but the park is rarely full.

INDOOR LODGING

GrandStay Hotel & Suites *908 S. Kniss Ave., Luverne; 507-449-4949; grandstayhospitality .com/find-a-hotel/locations/luverne/overview; $93–$129/night*

The GrandStay is a newer hotel on the south edge of Luverne that offers a variety of accommodations if you need a roof over your head during your trip to Rock County. It has an indoor pool to keep the kids occupied, and suites with full kitchens are available. The hotel also has bicycles to borrow, even if you aren't a guest there (see the "Biking" section on the next page).

Hillcrest Motel *210 W. Virginia St., Luverne; 507-283-2363; hillcrestmotel.com; about $55–$65/night*

If the Grandstay is too fancy for your tastes, try the Hillcrest, a nice little motel right off the main drag in the middle of town. No online reservations are available, though, so you'll have to call to check availability and specific rates.

HIKING ☁

You can walk or take a short drive from the Blue Mounds campground southwest to the parking lot where the park's main trails begin. Three trails head south toward the park's visitor center, just under 2 miles away. The **Mound Trail** is your best option if you want to hike along the prairie, adjacent to the park's bison range. The **Upper Cliffline Trail** runs on top of the cliffs, while the **Lower Cliffline Trail** sits below them; a side trail connects the two about midpoint if you don't want to go all the way to the

■ This rock formation gives Blue Mounds its name.

visitor center. The Lower Cliffline is paved and doubles as a bike trail; otherwise, the trails are a mix of grass and dirt. There is obviously an elevation change between the top of the cliffs and the bottom, but otherwise the trail is relatively flat.

If you choose Lower Cliffline Trail, a spur trail about 0.2 mile from the end will take you past the park's historic quarry area and on to the visitor center. If you stay on the pavement you will end up in the small parking lot used by rock climbers.

The visitor center has a parking lot if you choose to start there and hike in the opposite direction. To reach the center, you'll need to exit the campground area of the park, drive south on US 75, and turn east on County Road 8. Whether you hike

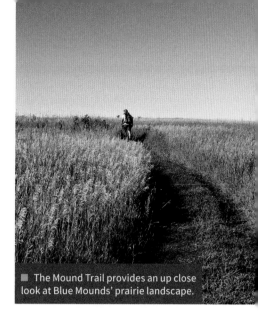

■ The Mound Trail provides an up close look at Blue Mounds' prairie landscape.

to the visitor center or drive there, it's a required stop. Nearby is a 1,250-foot-long wall of rocks and boulders (no more than 5 feet tall). These rocks are aligned in an east–west direction, and while it is not known how or why they were built, on the first day of spring and fall the sunrise and sunset are lined up on this formation. Perhaps this is Minnesota's version of Stonehenge?

When you're at the visitor center, it's worth following the signs to **Eagle Rock**, a short distance uphill from the building. The rock is a high point that allows you to see the prairie and Luverne—and, in fact, all the way to Iowa to the south and South Dakota to the west.

Another hiking option, especially if you're interested in seeing bison, is the **Western Loop Trail**, which begins near the visitor center. The trail runs just under 2 miles and often provides glimpses of the park's bison herd as they congregate in the far southwestern corner of the park.

BIKING 🚲

If you want to bike near the state park but elect not to travel with your cycle, check with the bicycle loan program, which was started in 2017 by the Luverne Chamber of Commerce in cooperation with the Grandstay Hotel and local bike repairman Ken Petersen. Twelve bikes (eight for adults and four for kids) are available at the hotel (see address and contact info on the previous page) and can be borrowed free of charge for up to 24 hours at a time. A driver's license or credit card is required, and no helmets are provided (so please bring your own).

The most popular route in the area is the 6-mile **Blue Mound Trail,** of which about a third is within the park. It is a good example of trails that have been championed by towns near Minnesota state parks, offering a fun and easy way for park visitors to get to know the local area and sample its commercial offerings, while at the same time providing more recreational opportunities for residents. You can access the Blue Mound Trail from near the park's visitor center or its main entrance and bike it all the way to Luverne. You can also start biking in Luverne by parking at Redbird Field near the trailhead at the intersection of Main Street and Blue Mound Avenue, and then take the trail straight north to the park. A map of the trail can be found at cityofluverne.org/trails. The website also has up-to-date information on the status of the Luverne Loop, a new 7-mile bike trail that is being constructed in three phases.

Casey Jones Trail *13 miles*

If you want a longer bike ride, consider driving about 22 miles north from Blue Mounds to Pipestone, where you can pick up the Casey Jones Trail. The trail runs 13 miles east, just past the town of Woodstock at the Pipestone–Murray county line. The first 5 miles are paved; the section from there into Woodstock is expected to be paved soon. A map of the trail can be found at files.dnr.state.mn.us/maps/state _trails/casey_jones.pdf.

> ***Directions*** From Blue Mounds State Park, take US 75 north to 101st Street (MN 30) and turn left. In about 4 blocks turn right on 8th Avenue NE. The trailhead is on the right, just south of the intersection with MN 23.

■ Eagle Rock

CLIMBING 🧗

The rock formation at Blue Mounds makes it a popular spot for climbing; although, as this area is in the far corner of Minnesota, with few other climbing opportunities nearby, *popular* is a relative term. Let's just say that with about 200 climbing routes at Blue Mounds, climbers never have to stand in line.

The climbs are rarely higher than 50 feet and are rated in difficulty from 5.4 to 5.12. There are no bolted routes.

A good online source of information about climbing specifics at Blue Mounds is mountainproject.com/area/105812716 ./blue-mounds-state-park-luverne.

Directions You can access the climbing spots from the hiking and bike trails in the park, but the easiest way to get there is to drive to a small parking lot near the southeast end of the park, off CR 8. If you exit the park from the main entrance, turn right on US 75 and then east on 141st Street, which is also CR 8. Stay on the road until it veers northeast and watch for the parking lot just as the road starts to straighten out. You'll find signage near the parking lot that will help point you to the climbing routes.

■ Upper Cliffline Trail at Blue Mounds State Park

OTHER ACTIVITIES ➕

Blue Mounds State Park offers a 90-minute Prairie and Bison Tour three times a day on Fridays, Saturdays, and Sundays between Memorial Day and Labor Day. An open-sided van that can hold 12 passengers drives through areas of the park not accessible to private vehicles. A guide discusses the bison herd, the prairie, and the park's history. Adult tickets are $10 and children's tickets are $6. Reservations are recommended. For more information or to make reservations, visit dnr.state.mn.us/state_parks/blue_mounds/prairie-and-bison-tour or reservemn.usedirectcom/MinnesotaWeb/Activities/ProgramsAndTours.

RAINY DAY 🌧

Brandenburg Gallery *213 E. Luverne St., Luverne; 507-283-1884; jimbrandenburg.com*

It's hard to find a gallery this nice anywhere, let alone in a little town like Luverne. Fortunately for Luverne, nature photographer Jim Brandenburg decided to honor his hometown by opening one of his two galleries (the other one is in Ely) here. Jim is certainly the most famous photographer to come out of Minnesota, with decades of stunning work for *National Geographic* and a series of books, including *Chased by the Light*. The Luverne gallery contains images that focus on the prairie, with profits from the venture used to promote, preserve, and expand the local prairie. The gallery is located in the Rock County Veterans Memorial Building, one of many buildings in town made of Sioux quartzite, which stands adjacent to the Rock County Courthouse.

Herried Military Museum *213 E. Luverne St., Luverne; 507-283-4061; luvernechamber.com/m/listing/view/user304*

Housed in the same building as the Brandenburg Gallery, the museum opened in 2009 and focuses on the stories of Rock County residents who served in World War II. The museum has since been expanded to include displays ranging from the Civil War to today's War on Terror. It's open weekdays 8 a.m.–5 p.m. and Saturdays 10 a.m.–5 p.m.

Palace Theatre   *104 E. Main St., Luverne; 507-283-4339; palacetheatre.us*

This beautifully renovated theatre hosts live events, movies, and performances by the Green Earth Players. A summer cinema series offers movies for kids.

FOOD AND DRINK 🍔

Sterling's Cafe & Grille   *107 E. Main St., Luverne; 507-449-0220; sterlingsluverne.com*

Sterling's is located in the Arcade Building, the most distinctive building on Main Street, a beautiful restoration project completed through the work of the Luverne Historical Preservation Committee and a nonprofit called Luverne Initiatives for Tomorrow (LIFT). The Sioux quartzite facade was returned to its original glory, and the restaurant features historical photos. It also serves up some tasty baby back ribs and a fine steak stroganoff.

The Bluestem   *1202 S. Kniss Ave., Luverne; 507-449-2583; the-bluestem.com*

You'll rarely find a menu as creative in a town the size of Luverne. The Swedish bison meatloaf (the meatloaf is Swedish, not the bison) and brisket nachos are great examples. They also offer gluten-free options.

Take 16 Brewing Company   *509 E. Main St., Luverne; 855-582-5316; take16beer.com*

These days, no town big or small in Minnesota is complete without a local craft brewer. Take 16's taproom is the same place where they brew and package their beer, which is distributed throughout the Midwest. The taproom is open only Thursdays and Fridays 4–10 p.m. and Saturdays noon–10 p.m. Nonalcoholic drinks and snacks are also available.

GEAR AND RESUPPLY 🛒

Ken's Bike Shop   *211 N. Freeman Ave., Luverne; 507-350-9660*

If your bike needs a quick tweak, Ken's Bike Shop is the only game in town—and for a long way around, as a matter of fact. The shop, which is behind Ken Petersen's residence, does not sell bikes but does offer adjustments and repairs. Ken is not always there, so it's not a bad idea to call before you stop by.

The tepees at Blue Mounds State Park offer a unique camping experience

If you need a relaxing adventure, try floating down the Root River.

ROOT RIVER

Anyone who lives in Minnesota knows what "up north" means. It's the direction most people from the Twin Cities (and elsewhere) head for outdoor weekends. But here's a suggestion: Be different. Think about heading southeast.

For one thing, you'll avoid the extended northbound traffic jams on I-35 or US 10, which means you won't start your weekend with skyrocketing blood pressure. But the best part about going southeast is that within 2 hours of leaving the cities, you'll be in the middle of one of the most picturesque areas of the state. And once there, relaxed and ready for action, you can pick and choose from a wide variety of activities that range from relaxing to taxing.

The dominating presence in this area is the Root River, and not just because of the paddling opportunities it affords. Most of the 60 miles of multiuse trail found here hug the Root's riverbank, providing a scenic route for bicyclists, walkers, and in-line skaters in warm weather and cross-country skiers in winter. The trail is dotted with nine small towns, each with its own unique charm.

If you visit here, resist the urge to try to take it all in during one trip. There are too many miles (water or land) to cover here in 48 hours, and the trail towns deserve more than a cursory stop. But we're pretty sure that once you've seen southeastern Minnesota, your first visit won't be your last.

Areas included: Root River State Trail, Harmony–Preston Valley State Trail, Root River State Water Trail, Forestville/Mystery Cave State Park, Historic Forestville, Lanesboro, Fountain, Preston, Harmony, Whalan, Peterson, Rushford, Houston

Adventures: Camping, biking, paddling, tubing, hiking, cross-country skiing

Directions: From the Twin Cities, this trip should take you about 2 hours. Take US 52 south out of Saint Paul and through Rochester. Take Exit 51 to get to US 63 S, heading toward Stewartville. The highway will turn east south of Racine. When you reach Spring Valley, take MN 16 to Fillmore County Road 5 and turn south, then go east on CR 118 until you reach Maple Road, and follow the directions into the park.

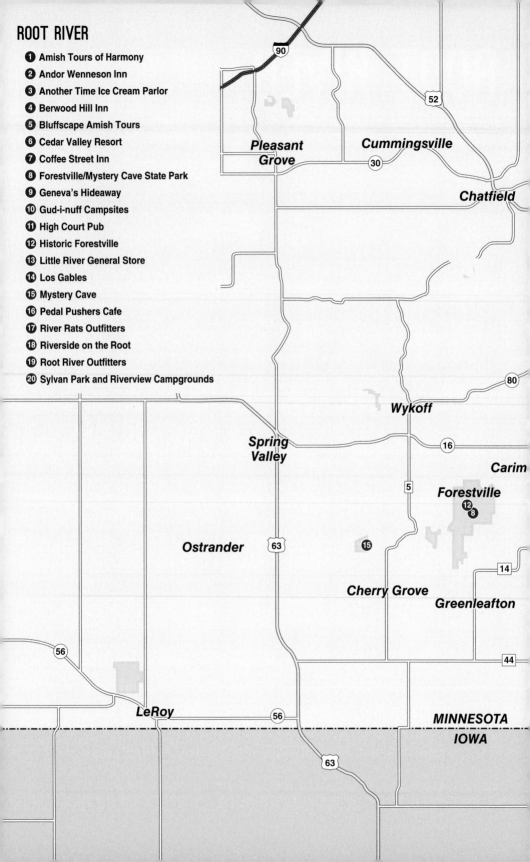

ROOT RIVER

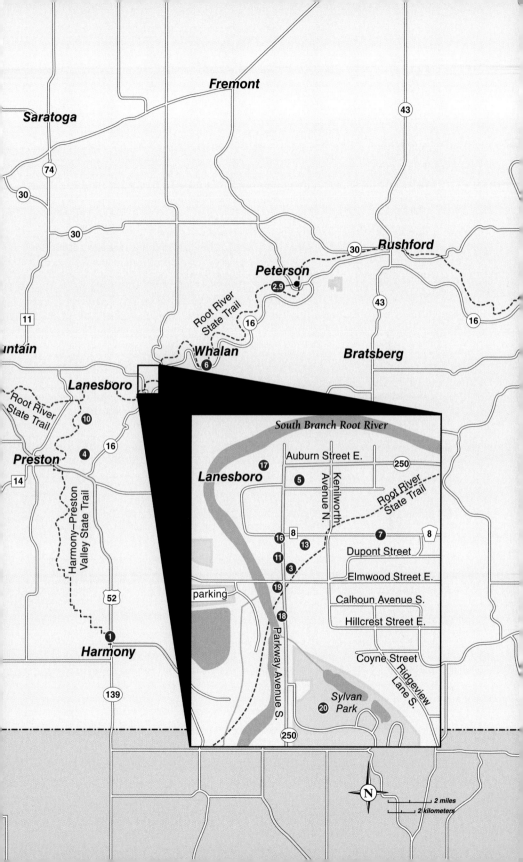

Fremont

Saratoga

43

74

30

30

Rushford

30

Peterson

11

Root River State Trail

2,9

43

16

16

Whalan

6

Bratsberg

Lanesboro

Root River State Trail

10

4

16

Preston

14

Harmony–Preston Valley State Trail

52

1

Harmony

139

South Branch Root River

Auburn Street E.

17

Lanesboro

5

Kenilworth Avenue N.

250

Root River State Trail

16

8

7

8

13

Dupont Street

11

3

Elmwood Street E.

parking

19

Calhoun Avenue S.

18

Hillcrest Street E.

Coyne Street

Ridgeview Lane S.

Parkway Avenue S.

Sylvan Park

20

250

N

2 miles

2 kilometers

LODGING 🛖

TOP PICK

FORESTVILLE/MYSTERY CAVE STATE PARK (MINNESOTA DEPARTMENT OF NATURAL RESOURCES) *21071 County Road 118, Preston; 507-352-5111; dnr.state .mn.us/state_parks/park.html?id=spk00148. $17–$23/night ($8 more for sites with electric hookups) for drive-in sites, 73 sites, 23 with electric hookups, open for camping early April–late November (check with park for specific dates); $60–$70 for camper cabins, 5 camper cabins, all with heat and electricity, open year-round; reservations required; sites have picnic table, fire ring, grill, flush and vault toilets, water, showers; state park permit required ($35 annual, $7 daily).*

Both state-owned and private campgrounds abound in this area of Minnesota. But there's no better spot than Forestville, also the closest state park to Lanesboro, 15 miles away.

Forestville has attractions you won't find anywhere else in the state. You could—if you wanted—spend an entertaining weekend without ever leaving the park.

To start with, Forestville is a very good place to pitch a tent and stretch your legs. Much of the campground is heavily wooded, with most of the nonelectric sites offering plenty of privacy, especially in the A loop (sites A8–A20 are the best). There are 20 miles of hiking trails, although because Forestville has the highest equine use of any Minnesota state park, 17 of those miles double as a horse path. The trails have only minor elevation changes, so the hiking is easy for people of all abilities. The 2-mile trail to Big Spring, accessed from the parking lot west of the C camping loop, is a scenic jaunt that includes a bridge over the Root River, the perfect place to take a break.

In addition, three renowned trout fishing creeks converge in the park, offering excellent angling opportunities. If you plan to fish, though, make sure you have a Minnesota fishing license and trout stamp.

Even after all that, you've yet to experience what makes this park special—Mystery Cave and Historic Forestville. You'll find information on both in our "Other Adventures" section on pages 128–130.

> **Directions** Note that while the park's address is listed as in Preston, it is actually about at the midpoint between Preston and Spring Valley. Also, be careful if you rely on a GPS in your car for directions—it may send you to a road north of the park with a closed bridge. The directions below avoid that obstacle.

> **To Lanesboro from Forestville** This is a 15-minute trip. Go northwest on CR 118 until you reach CR 11. Head north on 11 until you reach MN 16 and turn east. Turn southeast on US 52 and then northeast on MN 16 to Lanesboro.

BACKUP BASE CAMPS

Sylvan Park and Riverview Campgrounds *202 Parkway Ave. S., Lanesboro; 507-467-3722; lanesboro.com/list/category/campgrounds-5; $20–$30/night, May 1–November 30, 103 sites, including 60 tent-only and 43 camper-only sites; reservations not required; flush toilets, water, coin-operated showers, fire rings.*

If you prefer to access recreational opportunities with little or no driving, these city-operated Lanesboro campgrounds are located right in a park in the middle of town, with bluffs as a backdrop, accommodating tent campers as well as RVers. It's just a short walk to both bike and water trails. You will not get the private, wooded experience of Forestville—the campgrounds are largely open grass fields, so there isn't much to separate you from your neighbor. But if you're fine with a lack of solitude, these campgrounds will put you close to everything in Lanesboro, and any kids in your party with surely appreciate the amenities offered in the park, including playground equipment.

Gud-i-nuff Campsites *23653 Hickory Road, Lanesboro; 507-421-8008; gudinuffcampsites .shutterfly.com; $15–$20/night, 10 campsites; open spring–fall (contact owner for specific dates); reservations not required; vault toilets, no running water.*

If primitive camping is more to your liking but you want to stay near Lanesboro, this operation offers tent-only, spacious campsites on a secluded bluff overlooking the Root River on 40 acres of private land. The owners say they strive to offer "peaceful seclusion." Visit the website for detailed descriptions and photos of each site.

> **Directions** Gud-i-nuff is located about 6 miles outside of Lanesboro. Head southwest out of Lanesboro on MN 16. Turn west on Hickory Road, then go north.

INDOOR LODGING

Lanesboro bills itself as the Bed-and-Breakfast Capital of Minnesota, and it's not just marketing hype. There are a dozen B&Bs in the Lanesboro area, and even more in the other towns along the river. Here are two in Lanesboro and another up the road in Peterson:

Coffee Street Inn *305 Coffee St. E., Lanesboro; 507-467-2674; coffeestreetinn.com; $99–$325/night, varies seasonally; nine rooms and suites, open year-round, with a two-night minimum stay on weekends May–October.*

Lanesboro's main drag is Parkway Avenue, which can get (relatively) busy at times. This B&B sits off the beaten path on Coffee Street, on the northern end of town, with a beautiful view of the bluffs to the north and easy access to the bike trail. A short walk gets you to restaurants, shopping, and entertainment. The Java guest room is on the first floor with access directly off the garden patio, with a queen-size four-poster bed. If you need more room, try the Cappuccino, a two-story suite that also has direct access off the garden patio and has a nice front porch with a view of the bluffs; it sleeps up to eight people and has a living room with hardwood floors and a fully equipped kitchen.

Berwood Hill Inn *22139 Hickory Road, Lanesboro; 612-867-3614; berwood.com; $135–$215/night, varies seasonally; eight rooms and one separate cottage, open year-round, with a two-night minimum stay on weekends May–October.*

If you don't need to access Lanesboro by foot from your lodging, or prefer something of a country estate feel, consider the Berwood. Set high on 200 acres, this inn offers beautiful views of the Root River Valley, with award-winning gardens and acres of woodlands. The Berwood has eight rooms in the main house, but the private Garden Cottage may be the most fun place for two people to stay on the property, as long as you don't mind walking up to the house to use the bathroom (it is private). If you want a little more room and proximity to the facilities, check out the Owl's Nest, which takes up the entire top floor of the house and has a whirlpool bath to help soothe the muscles you've been working all day.

Andor Wenneson Inn *425 Prospect St., Peterson; 507-875-2587; andorwennesoninn.com; $85–$139/night, varies seasonally; nine rooms, open year-round, with a two-night minimum stay on weekends May–October.*

This inn, built by local businessman Andor Wenneson, served railroad travelers in the early part of the 20th century and, after sitting empty for a few years, was restored in 1994 to honor its history, with antiques and period furnishings. The carriage house, with four rooms, was added in 2001. Try the Loft, which has a private entrance on the second floor of the carriage house, or Florence's Room on the first floor, with six windows providing plenty of natural light.

SOUTHERN MINNESOTA BONUS

If you're visiting this area during summer, we have a special treat for you. Heard the joke about Minnesota's state bird being the mosquito? It's true that the warm-weather pest can ruin the best adventure weekend almost anywhere in the state—but not in southern Minnesota. Yes, you will encounter the little buggers, but generally only in small numbers. Because the glaciers that came through the state millions of years ago missed most of this area, there are few of the lakes and ponds—standing water—that mosquitoes need to breed. And that's a good thing!

BIKING

It may be going out on a limb to declare that Minnesota's biking trails rival any in the country, but it's a claim we're comfortable making. You can find first-class paved trails in any area of the state, often the result of small towns recognizing the positive economic impact of building routes to attract recreation-minded Minnesotans. These efforts were often made easier by the large number of abandoned railroad lines that could be converted into bike trails.

There is no better example of this in the state than the Root River trail system, which includes both the 42-mile **Root River State Trail** and the 18-mile **Harmony–Preston Valley State Trail**. The two trails meet just north of Preston.

Biking across the Root River in Lanesboro

You will not find a prettier trail anywhere (honestly!), as you wind through the old railroad corridor along the river, with limestone bluffs, wildflower fields, and farms spread out before you. More than 40 wooden bridges are sprinkled along the trail, often with nearby benches and picnic areas that allow you to take in a view of the river while you rest your bones.

While some ambitious cyclists might pedal the entire trail in the course of a long weekend, the Root River vibe is much more relaxed. This is a trail made for meandering, and you'll find more families pedaling along than speed racers. The nine communities along the route have gone out of their way to welcome trail users, encouraging them to rest up and refuel at visitor centers, ice-cream shops, and city parks. Lanesboro has the most attractions, but each of the other eight towns also caters to visiting cyclists. For a list of museums, shops, and other facilities in the towns along the trail, visit rootrivertrail.com.

In general, the trail is relatively flat, given its railroad history (only the far east and west portions were not built on a railroad bed), making it suitable to family bike trips, wheelchair accessibility, and in-line skating. But there are exceptions. The eastern section of the Root River Trail, about halfway between Rushford and Houston, has steep portions, as does a good part of the southern third of the Harmony–Preston segment. If you end in Fountain, the last segment will get your heart pumping.

One of the best stretches of the trail is the 27 miles from Lanesboro east to Peterson, with the path shaded by a canopy of trees along the riverbank as it gently winds its way north and south; if that distance is too much, pick a spot partway and then turn around. Six small picnic areas along this portion of the trail make it easy to pick the right spot for lunch or a water break. Less than 5 miles from Lanesboro, you'll run into Whalan, the smallest town on the trail. You might be tempted to stop at the Aroma Pie Shop on the way out, but a slice of cherry might be better on the way back, if you can be so disciplined.

If you're looking for something a little more open to the sky, you'll find it on the 6.5 miles of trail between Fountain and the junction with the Harmony–Preston Valley State Trail to the east. You'll also experience less traffic here than to the east.

If you're wary of the grade going west into Fountain, and you have two vehicles, consider parking one at the Isinours Forestry Unit near the east end of this segment, then drive the other to the starting point in Fountain and cycle back to the first one.

A guide to the Root River and Harmony–Preston Valley State Trails is available at files.dnr.state.mn.us/maps/state_trails/rootriver_harmonypreston.pdf. A TrailLink map is also online at traillink.com/trail-maps/root-river-state-trail.

PADDLING ⊗

Just as the bike trails surrounding Lanesboro are family-friendly, so is the water that runs alongside most of the trail. The winding 80-mile **Root River** has a slow to mod-

■ The Root River's slow–moderate flow makes it family-friendly.

erate flow, with no rapids to speak of, so if you're floating with the current, don't expect to set any speed records. River levels vary according to rainfall, but generally peak in early June; in years of light rainfall, shallow areas can occasionally be a problem.

As long as you're moving slow, enjoy the view. It's as good as it is from the trail—maybe better—because you have the opportunity to lie back and relax. You'll see farmland and prairie in areas, but bluffs will tower over you as well.

There are eight official spots along the waterway to put in boats, most of them near the towns on the trail, where you will also find plenty of businesses that rent canoes, kayaks, or tubes and will shuttle you a distance so you can float back to your vehicle (see the "Gear and Resupply" section on page 131).

If you're interested in making your trip an overnight adventure, there are private campgrounds along the river, as well as five first-come, first-served sites operated by the Minnesota Department of Natural Resources.

For more information, visit dnr.state.mn.us/watertrails/rootriver. The official state water trail guide to the Root River can be found at files.dnr.state.mn.us/maps/canoe_routes/root.pdf.

OTHER ADVENTURES ⊕

Historic Forestville *21899 County Road 188, Preston; 507-765-2785; $8 adults, $6 children ages 5–17, free for children under 5; open Saturdays May 5–25, Thursday–Sunday May 26– September 3, and Saturdays only until end of October.*

In this era of video games and online entertainment, it may be a little amazing that something like Historic Forestville has survived, what with its old buildings and costumed guides portraying residents and workers from 1899. But the place carries on because they do what they do so well. (A jaded teenager may pretend they don't find it fascinating, but don't believe them.)

It helps that Historic Forestville is the real deal. The town sprung up about 160 years ago but faded a few years later when it was bypassed by the railroad. Thomas Meighen's general store remained, though, until 1910. When it closed, the unsold goods (from canned food to clothing) were left in the store and preserved by the Minnesota Historical Society.

Authentic? As we say in Minnesota, "you betcha."

The Historic Forestville guides play members of the Meighan family, as well as employees, explaining what it was like to live and work in a tiny Minnesota community at the turn of the century. My prediction? Kids will have enough fun that they'll forget it's educational (and so will adults).

> **Directions** Head out of the park on Maple Road, toward CR 118. Take 118 about 1.3 miles to Historic Forestville.

Amish Tours of Harmony *94 2nd St., Harmony; 507-866-2303; amish-tours.com; $25 for adults, $20 for teens, $8 for kids ages 4–12; operates seasonally*

Bluffscape Amish Tours *102 Beacon St. E., Lanesboro; 507-467-3070; bluffscape.com; $30 for adults, $25 for teens, $10 for kids ages 6–12; operates seasonally*

As you travel through southeast Minnesota, you will undoubtedly pass Amish buggies along the roads and highways. These tours offer the chance to learn about the Amish way of life, stopping at Amish farms while a tour guide talks about Amish culture and heritage.

Mystery Cave *21071 County Road 118, Preston; 507-937-3251; dnr.state.mn.us/mystery_ cave; $10–$80 admission; reservations can be made online at reservations1.usedirect.com /MinnesotaWebHome/Activities/programsandtours.aspx or by calling 866-857-2757.*

Ever been on a cave tour that was pretty cheesy? "Mystery Cave" would be the name for one like that, right? Well, that's not the case here. This is a cave tour done right, maybe because the place is owned and operated by the state, not someone mostly interested in selling tchotchkes from a gift shop.

Mystery Cave, discovered in 1937, is the longest cave in Minnesota, more than 13 miles underground. Tours are led by state park naturalists who, in our experience, know what they're talking about. Most people opt for the 1-hour scenic tour ($10 for youth, $15 for adults), which involves walking on a paved trail and metal bridges for less than a mile. This guided tour provides the best overall cave experience, offering excellent views of cave mineral deposits illuminated by artificial lighting.

But if you really want to have fun, go for the lantern tour ($18 per person, no one under 8 allowed). This tour is also 1 hour long, but lanterns provide the only lighting, and you'll cover more ground going down long, straight passages. You'll get more in-depth interpretation than on the scenic tour, and although it's more physically challenging, it's nothing an adult in decent physical shape can't handle.

Two-hour photo ($40 per person) and geology ($23, ages 8 and above) tours are also available, and then there's the granddaddy 4-hour wild caving tour ($80, no one under 13), in which you crawl on hands and knees through undeveloped portions of the cave. That's probably not for anyone who suffers from claustrophobia! (Wild caving and photo tours must be reserved in advance.)

Directions From Forestville, take CR 118 west to CR 5. Turn left and follow CR 5 south 2 miles. Turn right on 180th Street and go west about 0.75 mile. At the next intersection, turn right on Old Cave Road and proceed north 0.5 mile to the Mystery Cave Entrance Road on the left.

FOOD AND DRINK ☕

Riverside on the Root *109 Parkway Ave. S., Lanesboro; 507-467-3663; riversideontheroot.com; operates seasonally*

Any adventure weekend should include spending as little time indoors as possible, even when dining, right? You can eat indoors at Riverside on the Root if you'd like, but a better option is relaxing on the patio, where you'll find live entertainment Friday–Sunday evenings during the summer. This operation has been family owned since 1992.

Pedal Pushers Cafe *121 Parkway Ave. N., Lanesboro; 507-467-1050; pedalpusherscafe.com; open Wednesday–Sunday*

Need some caffeine for that bike ride? This cafe roasts its own beans on site (and supplies beans to a lot of the B&Bs in town). But its locally sourced food makes it stand out as well. Try the Norwegian meatballs or, if so inclined, the liver and onions. Good gluten-free options can be found here as well, including the Korean BBQ lettuce wraps and Cobb salad.

Historic Forestville

High Court Pub *109 Parkway Ave. N., Lanesboro; 507-467-2782; highcourtpub.com*

The High Court Pub is the first place I visited in Lanesboro years ago, and I've kept going back. A change in ownership in 2015 has injected some new energy, with an emphasis on craft beers and artisan flatbreads. It's a good spot for live music.

Another Time Ice Cream Parlor *100 Parkway Ave. N., Lanesboro; 507-467-3556*

Don't pass through Lanesboro without stopping for ice cream here—or fudge or truffles!

Los Gables *122 US 52, Fountain; 507-268-1020; losgables.com*

This restaurant on the main intersection in Fountain has gone through some iterations over the years, but the current emphasis on Mexican cuisine is a winner. If you're looking for calories before a bike ride, try the huevos con chorizo or breakfast fajita wrap.

GEAR AND RESUPPLY 🛒

Root River Outfitters *101 Parkway Ave. N., Lanesboro; 507-467-3400; rootriveroutfitters.com*

This centrally located outfitter rents bikes, canoes, kayaks, and tubes (shuttle available).

Little River General Store *105 Coffee St., Lanesboro; 507-467-2943; lrgeneralstore.net*

If your bike needs a quick tune-up or repair, this is the place to go. Little River also rents bikes, canoes, kayaks, and tubes (shuttle available).

River Rats Outfitters *103 Rivers Edge Road, Lanesboro; 507-429-7202; riverratsoutfitters.com*

River Rats rents canoes and kayaks (shuttle available).

Cedar Valley Resort/Outfitters *905 Bench St., Whalan; 507-467-9000; cedarvalleyresort.com*

This resort rents a variety of bikes, including child trailers. They'll also shuttle you and your bikes to different points on the trail.

> **Directions** Whalan is located about 5 miles from Lanesboro. From Lanesboro, take Coffee Street east to MN 16 and follow it to Whalan. When you arrive in town, turn left on Main Street and follow it to Bench Street.

Geneva's Hideaway *318 Mill St., Peterson; 507-875-7733; genevashideaway.com*

Geneva's not only operates a small hotel, but it also rents canoes, kayaks, and tubes and will shuttle you up the river so you can float back to your vehicle. It's not a bad idea to call for reservations if you're interested in renting on a weekend.

> **Directions** Peterson is located about 15 miles from Lanesboro. From Lanesboro, take Coffee Street east to MN 16, follow it past Whalan and up to Peterson. When you arrive in town, turn left on Mill Street and follow it to Geneva's, which will be on the right side of the road.

Palisade Head near Silver Bay

SILVER BAY

The middle part of the North Shore of Lake Superior in Minnesota, stretching from Silver Bay up to the Schroeder area, might just take the cake for having the most outdoor adventure opportunities of any chapter in this guide. You have three state parks to choose from, all unique in their own right, plus state forests with campgrounds. Hiking trails abound in and around all three parks, including popular sections of the Superior Hiking Trail (SHT), offering some of the finest scenery—notably a series of spectacular waterfalls—anywhere in the state. There is access to the big lake at numerous points, whether you want to paddle or just stick your toe in the water of the largest freshwater lake (by volume) on the continent. You could probably spend the entire weekend at Tettegouche (pronounced tet-a-goosh) State Park and never run out of things to do. But then you'd miss the sights of the Temperance River, the rugged trails at George Crosby Manitou State Park, and . . . well, you get the idea. Yes, you will have some decisions to make here. The first one is just what you're going to be able to cover in a weekend. The second is when you're going to come back.

Areas included: Tettegouche State Park, George Crosby Manitou State Park, Temperance River State Park, Gitchi-Gami State Trail, Silver Bay

Adventures: Camping, hiking, biking, climbing, exploring

Directions: From the Forest Lake area north of the Twin Cities, take I-35 north about 128 miles. In Duluth, turn right on MN 61 (London Road) and continue about 52 miles to Silver Bay. (You can also take the North Shore Scenic Drive, the old MN 61 between Duluth and Two Harbors, which will add a bit of time to your trip but will give you plenty of views of Lake Superior and some nice places to stop. You can choose that route as you reach the northeast edge of Duluth.)

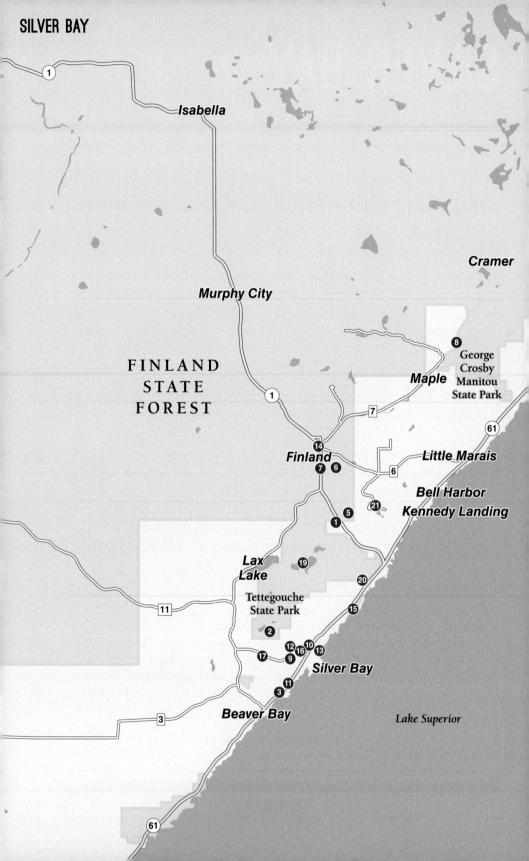

SILVER BAY

SUPERIOR
NATIONAL
FOREST

Lutsen

61

④ Temperance
River State Park Tofte

18

Schroeder

Taconite
Harbor

Lake Superior

❶ Baptism River Inn Bed and Breakfast
❷ Bean and Bear Lakes Loop
❸ Beaver Bay Sports
❹ Carlton Peak
❺ Eckbeck Campground
❻ Finland Campground
❼ Four Seasons Supper Club
❽ George Crosby Manitou State Park
❾ Gitchi-Gami State Trail
⑩ Mariner Motel
⑪ North Shore Scenic Cruises
⑫ Northwoods Family Grille
⑬ Onyx (Black) Beach
⑭ Our Place
⑮ Palisade Head
⑯ Rocky Taconite
⑰ Silver Bay Trailhead
⑱ Temperance River State Park
⑲ Tettegouche Camp
⑳ Tettegouche State Park
㉑ Wolf Ridge Environmental
   Learning Center

MINNESOTA
WISCONSIN

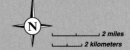

TOP PICK

TETTEGOUCHE STATE PARK (MINNESOTA DEPARTMENT OF NATURAL RESOURCES) *5702 MN 61, Silver Bay; 218-353-8800; dnr.state.mn.us/state_parks /park.html?id=spk00269. $17–$23/night ($8 more for sites with electric hookups) for drive-, walk-, and cart-in sites, 42 sites, 22 with electric hookups, 14 cart-in, 6 walk-in; reservations required; sites have picnic table, fire ring, grill, showers, flush and vault toilets; state park permit required ($35 annual, $7 daily).*

I've spent more than 60 nights camping at Tettegouche over the years, and it never fails to show me something new when I visit. If you love the outdoors, this park is simply a dream place to stay. You can go deep into the woods, hiking through forests of yellow birch, spruce, red oak, and maple trees. If you wander closer to Lake Superior, such as to the Baptism River from the spacious and well-appointed park visitor center (new in 2014), you'll be amid birch and aspen. There are scenic overlooks at Shovel Point and Palisade Head and roaring waterfalls just steps from the campground. Visitors will find 23 miles of hiking trails, including 15 miles groomed for cross-country skiing in the winter. Oh, and there's some of the best rock climbing in the state as well!

Camping at Tettegouche comes in all shapes and sizes. In recent years the park has reconfigured the campsites in the single-loop Baptism River Campground to be more RV-friendly, adding electrical hookups and making larger gravel pads for

■ The Baptism River flows into Lake Superior.

■ The cart-in campground at Tettegouche features incredible views of Lake Superior.

parking, but you'll find that most still offer better than average privacy, especially those on the outside of the loop (site 32 is about the only one I don't like much). There are six walk-in sites in this campground, but if everything other than the walk-ins are reserved, site W23 is only a few steps from the parking. W24 and W25 are in about 200–300 feet, but off by themselves and would make a good choice if you have a group large enough to need two sites and don't mind the short walk. The Lake Superior Cart-in Campground features a number of sites (E–K) with spectacular views of the lake. The cart-in sites require you to tote your gear in a cart from 0.3 to 0.6 mile over some hilly terrain. But they are enormous, remote sites, except for L, M, and N, which are clustered. Vault toilets are scattered around the area, and cart-in campers are welcome to use the showers and flush toilets at Baptism River Campground. Finally, the park has five backpack sites within its boundaries, but for camping purposes they are considered part of the SHT; so while there is no fee for the sites, they can't be reserved and must be shared.

■ Tettegouche is great for winter camping.

Directions From Silver Bay, it is about 4 miles north on MN 61 to the park.

BACKUP BASE CAMP

George Crosby Manitou State Park (Minnesota Department of Natural Resources)

7616 County Road 7, Finland; 218-353-8800; dnr.state.mn.us/state_parks/park.html?id=spk 00163. $13–$19/night for backpack sites, 21 sites; reservations required; fire ring, vault toilets near parking area, latrines near campsites; state park permit required ($35 annual, $7 daily).

George Crosby Manitou is the only state park on the North Shore that is not located right along MN 61—and it's the only one that requires you to backpack in to all the sites. But if you're looking for an unspoiled piece of wilderness in which to camp, Crosby Manitou definitely fits the bill. In line with the no-frills theme, there is no trail center here—the park is managed by the folks down at Tettegouche. The campsites are as far as 4.5 miles of rugged hiking from the parking area, but many backpackers are willing to stay at the more remote sites because of their location near the Manitou River and the views they afford (site 2, for example, is near a waterfall and overlook). If you'd rather not go so far, sites 20–22, which sit above Benson Lake, are less than a half mile from the parking lot, although they are not as secluded as those farther out. If you are going to stay in 20–22, and you want to make a short hike even shorter (maybe you'd like to haul in some camp chairs), there's a parking area at the beginning of the trail to the sites where you drop your stuff. Because there's no overnight parking there, you must return your vehicle to the main parking lot and walk back.

> **Directions from Tettegouche State Park** Go north on MN 61 from Tettegouche about 1 mile and turn left on MN 1 W. Go about 6 miles and turn right on Cramer Road (CR 7). You'll reach the park in about 7.5 miles.

Other camping options are available in this area as well, including **Temperance River State Park**, about 22 miles north of Tettegouche on MN 61. Also nearby are two **Finland State Forest** campgrounds, where the camping is rustic (no showers) but you don't need reservations—the **Eckbeck Campground** is 3 miles from Tettegouche and the **Finland Campground** is about 7 miles. Go to dnr.state.mn.us/state_forests /forest.html?id=sft00017 for more information on the state forest campgrounds.

■ Temperance River

INDOOR LODGING

Tettegouche Camp *5702 MN 61, Silver Bay; 218-353-8800; dnr.state.mn.us/state_parks /tettegouche/tettegouche_camp; $109–$159/night.*

Not many hoteliers could get away with charging up to $150 a night for accommodations that require a 2-mile walk from the car, with no bathroom or running water. Tettegouche can because there's more demand for cabins on this beautiful and remote property than there is supply. Four cabins are in the camp, three of which can sleep six people and one that sleeps two. There's also a roomy shelter and picnic area, and a bathroom with showers. Water is pumped from a spigot in the middle of the camp. Each cabin has a picnic table, fire ring with grill, and firewood. The nightly fee includes use of a canoe, paddles, and life vests.

The camp, originally called the Tettegouche Club, was built a century ago by a group of Duluth businessmen, who used it for hunting and fishing. After changing hands several times, it was sold to The Nature Conservancy and then to the State of Minnesota, which added the property to Baptism River State Park, which was renamed Tettegouche State Park in 1979.

> ***Directions from Tettegouche State Park*** Go north on MN 61 from the visitor center about 0.7 mile and turn left on MN 1 at Illgen City. In 4.3 miles turn left on Lax Lake Road. Drive 3.1 miles and park at the trailhead on the left side of the road.

Baptism River Inn Bed and Breakfast *6125 MN 1, Silver Bay; 218-353-0707; baptismriverinn.com; $149–$229/night*

Three rooms and a suite are available in this beautiful log lodge, far enough up MN 1 to feel remote, but close enough to all the Silver Bay area attractions. Check online for discounts for last-minute bookings.

Mariner Motel *46 Outer Drive, Silver Bay; 218-226-4488; call for room rates and reservations*

Many a SHT backpacker looking to get off the trail has taken rest at the Mariner (yours truly included), looking for basic accommodations at a budget price. There are single rooms as well as two- and three-bedroom units, some with kitchenettes.

HIKING ◔

There may be a broader array of hiking opportunities in the area covered by this chapter of the book than in any other.

George Crosby Manitou State Park *24 miles of trails*

You won't find any better backcountry trails in the state parks, but they aren't easy. These trails are rugged with plenty of elevation change. The one path that is mostly flat is the Benson Lake Trail, a loop under a mile long. You can add another couple of miles to that by taking either the Matt Willis or Beaver Bog Trails where they intersect the Benson Lake Trail, and then take the other back. You can also make a loop of under 3 miles by taking the Humpback Trail north from the parking lot to the Middle Trail, which will give you beautiful waterfall views—but it's a tough trail with lots of ups and downs.

■ On the trail at George Crosby Manitou State Park

Tettegouche State Park *23 miles of trails*

So many options here! Want something short? Take the 1-mile hike from the Tettegouche Visitor Center north to Shovel Point and back, with a view of Palisade Head to the west.

An even better choice is the High Falls Trail because it takes you right to stunning views of the highest waterfall completely within the boundaries of Minnesota. (It's 70 feet high; the 120-foot High Falls in Grand Portage State Park is part of the Canadian boundary). This is a round-trip of 3 miles, with lots of steep terrain and a few sets of stairs that never seem to end. But it is very much worth the trek. You can park at the visitor center and then walk south toward the river to pick up the trail, which goes up the east side of the Baptism River and back. You can take a spur trail to Two-Step Falls about a mile into the trip, but there is no river crossing there (as many people mistakenly assume). There is a crossing at High Falls that will take you about a third of a mile down the west side of the river to Tettegouche's Baptism River Campground, but there is no trail out of the campground to return to the visitor center—you have to go back the way you came. (Yes, if you're asking, you could skip the High Falls Trail altogether and just hike the trail from the campground to the falls and back. But that's not as much fun, and there are still steps!)

Finally, if you're interested in checking out Tettegouche Camp without staying overnight there, it's a 1.7-mike hike into the camp from the parking lot on Lax Lake Road. You're going to have steep hills both going in and coming back out.

Directions from Tettegouche State Park to Tettegouche Camp Go north on MN 61 from the visitor center about 0.7 mile and turn left on MN 1 at Illgen City. In 4.3 miles turn left on Lax Lake Road. Drive 3.1 miles and park at the trailhead on the left side of the road.

Bean and Bear Lakes Loop/Superior Hiking Trail *6.8 miles*

This trail starts in Silver Bay, about 4 miles south of Tettegouche State Park. The views of Bean and Bear Lakes from the hiking trail far above the water are among the most iconic on the SHT. Of course, to get those looks at this pair of lakes north of Silver Bay, you'll have to do some serious climbing. This isn't the easiest section of trail—in fact, it is considered one of the most challenging—but it may be the most rewarding.

There are a couple of options. The first, which totals about 6.8 miles, starts from the SHT parking lot on Penn Boulevard, on the far western edge of Silver Bay. You'll start on an ATV trail, but in a short distance you'll follow the SHT as it turns left and goes uphill. The trail crosses a couple more ATV trails and a gravel road before you hit the 1-mile mark. At the 1.8-mile mark, the trail comes to the junction of the Bean and Bear Lakes Loop. Go left at the intersection, heading toward the entrance to the Penn Creek campsite. In another half mile or so past the spur to the campsite, you'll turn northeast and reach the **Bean Lake** overlook. There are incredible views of the lakes as the trail continues along the cliffs. At the 3.4-mile mark, you pass the 150-yard spur trail that descends steeply to the Bear Lake campsite, and shortly thereafter, atop a bluff, you will reach an intersection. Don't follow the SHT east; instead turn right (south) onto the Twin Lakes Trail. In a little more than a half mile, you will come to another intersection. Turn right. The next intersection, also in about a half mile, is the first one you encountered on the way in; turn left (a right would take you to the Penn Creek campsite) here and head the 1.8 miles back to the parking lot.

Directions from Tettegouche State Park Go south on MN 61 from the visitor center for a little more than 4 miles. Turn right at mile marker 54.3, into Silver Bay on Outer Drive, which will turn into Penn Boulevard. (Don't forget to wave to Rocky Taconite!) In about 2 miles, as you're heading out of town, the Silver Bay Trailhead will be on your right.

(A second option to reach the Bean and Bear Lakes Loop adds close to another mile to the trip. Park in the lot for the Silver Bay Visitor Center/Historical Society, about a half mile in from MN 61 on Outer Drive, on the right. Follow the ATV trail from the parking lot for 0.7 mile, take a spur trail to the right, and go 1.6 miles to the intersection with the loop. Follow the loop either way—but be careful not to head off on the SHT where it departs from the loop trail—until you're back at the original intersection, then follow the "stem" the 2.3 miles back to the parking lot.)

Temperance River State Park
22 miles of trails

All those cars you see parked by the side of the road near the entrance to Temperance River State Park are there for a reason—short hikes to spectacular views. It may seem crowded in the areas right on either side of the highway, but any trail you take will thin out substantially after a

■ The Temperance River provides a scenic backdrop for hiking.

half mile or so. The waterfalls are the main attraction on the trails here, but there is plenty else to see along this gorge, including potholes full of swirling waters. There is quite a bit of elevation change on these routes, parts of which are shared with the SHT. Some suggestions:

- **Temperance River Gorge Trail,** 0.25 mile each way: From the parking area on the north side of MN 1, on the northeast side of the Temperance River, follow the trail to a deck where you can view the falls. Keep following the stairs to overlooks above the gorge.

- **Upper Falls,** 1 mile each way: From the parking area on the north side of MN 1, on the northeast side of the Temperance River, hike upstream past Hidden Falls and follow the stairs. Go left at the bike trail and take a right after the bridge. Follow the trail to the falls.

- **Carlton Peak,** 3 miles each way: Considering this trail leads to a peak, it is not as difficult as you might imagine—there are steep portions, but the ascent is relatively gradual. From the parking area on the north side of MN 1, on the northeast side of the Temperance River, follow the SHT. As you approach the peak, the trail begins a counterclockwise route around the peak, an area popular with rock climbers. A spur trail will take you to the summit.

BIKING

Mountain Biking *1.5 miles*

The trail and service road into Tettegouche Camp can be used by mountain bikers. See the "Hiking" section for directions.

Gitchi-Gami State Trail *2.3 and 3 miles*

A finished segment of trail runs 2.3 miles from Silver Bay to West Road in Beaver Bay. In Silver Bay, the trail starts at Outer Drive, across from the high school football field, adjacent to Rukavina Arena. Parking is available by the arena. In Beaver Bay, the trail starts at the trailhead near the intersection of MN 61 and Lax Lake Road.

Benson Lake at George Crosby Manitou State Park

A 3-mile segment of this bike trail runs between the towns of Schroeder and Tofte, with scenic views of Carlton Peak and about a half mile in Temperance River State Park that goes past the beautiful river gorge. Parking for this segment is available at the wayside rest in Schroeder and at the Tofte Town Park/Public Access on Lake Superior.

A map of the Gitchi-Gami State Trail bike route can be found online at dnr.state .mn.us/maps/state_trails/gitchi_gami.pdf. An interactive map is also available at ggta.org/map.php.

■ View of Shovel Point from Palisade Head

CLIMBING 🖊

Tettegouche is one of only four state parks that offer climbing. The climbing areas at **Shovel Point**, to the east of the park office, and at **Palisade Head**, south from the main park on MN 61, offer climbers some challenging routes and some of the best views in the entire state. There are three sets on climbing anchors along Shovel Point, which has dozens of routes. Palisade Head has five climbing areas and more than 100 routes, rated from 5.7 to 5.13.

If you're climbing in a state park, you'll need a (free) permit, which can be picked up at the park office.

A map of the climbing areas can be found here at dnr.state.mn.us/maps/state _parks/spk00269_climb.pdf.

> **Directions** The entrance to Palisade Head is about 1.5 miles south on MN 61 from the Tettegouche visitor center. It's a steep, narrow road up to the parking lot, so watch for cars going the other way.

OTHER ADVENTURES ➕

Palisade Head is a very cool place to visit even if you aren't climbing. The views of Shovel Point are incredible, and it's a nice place just to sit, relax, and take in the scenery. See the "Climbing" section for directions.

North Shore Scenic Cruises *Silver Bay Marina, 99 Beach Drive, Silver Bay; 218-464-6162; northshoresceniccruises.com; $25–$30/cruise*

A lot of North Shore visitors never venture onto the water. I'm not sure if that's because there's so much to do on land, or because there aren't a lot of options to get on the lake unless you have your own boat. For years, the *Grampa Woo* cruised the lake, but it ceased operations in 2006 and was replaced by North Shore Scenic Cruises, which offers daily 2-hour cruises either to Shovel Point or Split Rock Lighthouse. The cruises did not operate in 2018 but are expected to be back in 2019. When in operation, the cruises may be canceled if weather is an issue, so always call before you head to the marina.

Onyx Beach (also called Black Beach) *E. Lakeview Drive and Water Plant Road, Silver Bay*

This small beach is a nice spot on the water about 4 miles from Tettegouche, with an area for picnics. The beach is composed not of sand or onyx but instead of very fine taconite tailings.

RAINY DAY 😎

Wolf Ridge Environmental Learning Center *6282 Cranberry Road, Finland; 218-353-7414; wolf-ridge.org*

This learning center has been a treasure for generations of kids—and adults. It was the first environmental learning center in the United States to be accredited as a K–12 school and is recognized nationally and internationally as a leader in environmental education. It's open for drop-in visits as well, all weekdays but only some weekends (so call ahead). The folks at the office can tell you what's going on the day you visit and point you to the trails you can use to explore the 2,000-acre campus.

> **Directions** Follow MN 61 north from the park to CR 6 in Little Marais. Turn left on CR 6 and go about 4 miles to the Wolf Ridge driveway (Cranberry Road). Turn left into the driveway and follow it 2.5 miles to the main campus on the top of the ridge.

Explore Mic Mac Lake by canoe at Tettegouche State Park.

FOOD AND DRINK 🍽️

Northwoods Family Grille *6 Shopping Center Road, Silver Bay; 218-353-6060; northwoodsfamilygrille.com*

A few years ago, the Northwoods was a bit of a rundown coffee shop, where the food was decent (sometimes) but the ambience nonexistent. That's all changed. After a complete renovation, the Northwoods has a diverse and appealing menu, and there's finally an *atmosphere*. It's nice to finally have a decent place to eat in Silver Bay! It's a great place for a hearty breakfast, but there's a nice dinner menu, too, with excellent baby back ribs.

Our Place *5195 Heffelfinger Road, Finland; 218-353-7343*

This has long been a go-to place for a home-style meal following a long hike on the SHT. It's nothing fancy (fancy would be out of place in Finland), but the food is good, from the steaks to the Friday night fish fries, and the service is excellent.

Four Seasons Supper Club *6538 MN 1, Finland; 218-353-7371; four-seasons-supper-club .business.site*

I can't tell you how many times my wife and I drove by the Four Seasons, fooled by its unassuming exterior into believing . . . well, that can't really be a supper club, can it? Yes, it can and it is. It's a casual setting, to be sure, but once we stopped by, we found that the homemade meals (beef, fish, and chicken) hit the spot.

GEAR AND RESUPPLY 🛒

Beaver Bay Sports *4878 MN 61, Beaver Bay; 218-226-4666; beaverbaysports.com*

There are plenty of gear shops and outfitters up and down the North Shore, but not much in the area of Silver Bay. Beaver Bay Sports is your best choice, and they rent kayaks if you are so inclined. Otherwise, you're likely going to have to head south to Two Harbors or north to Tofte or Lutsen.

Gooseberry Falls is a popular North Shore attraction.

TWO HARBORS

This stretch of the North Shore of Lake Superior features some of the shore's must-see attractions, as well as (arguably) its best campground. Because Two Harbors is the first town you reach on the shore, and the largest, it can feel a little busy on popular weekends, and Gooseberry Falls State Park is often crowded when fall colors are at their peak, so plan accordingly. But for the most part, you should be able to explore to your heart's content without being elbow to elbow with your follow nature lovers. The best part of this section of the shore is that you can go calorie-burning by tackling long hikes or bike rides, or you can just chill by sitting on a pebble beach and skipping stones across the water of the world's largest freshwater lake. Either way, it's a paradise.

Areas included: (Two Harbors to Beaver Bay) Gooseberry Falls State Park, Split Rock Lighthouse State Park, Superior Hiking Trail, Lake Superior, Superior National Forest

Adventures: Camping, backpacking, biking, hiking, exploring, paddling

Directions: From the Forest Lake area north of the Twin Cities, take I-35 north about 128 miles. In Duluth, turn right on MN 61 (London Road) and continue about 24 miles. (You can also take the North Shore Scenic Drive, the old MN 61 between Duluth and Two Harbors, which will add a bit of time to your trip but will give you plenty of views of Lake Superior and some nice places to stop. You can choose that route as you reach the northeast edge of Duluth.)

TWO HARBORS

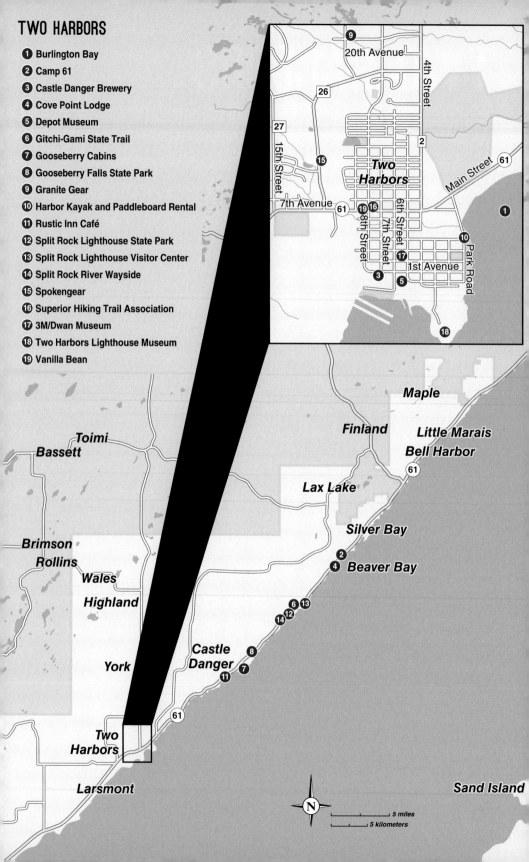

TOP PICK

SPLIT ROCK LIGHTHOUSE STATE PARK (MINNESOTA DEPARTMENT OF NATURAL RESOURCES) *3755 Split Rock Lighthouse Road, Two Harbors; 218-595-762; dnr.state.mn.us/state_parks. $17–$23/night for cart-in sites, 20 sites; $13–$19/night for backpack sites, 4 sites; $13/night for kayak sites, 1 site; reservations required; sites have picnic table, fire ring, grill, food storage boxes, flush and vault toilets, water, hot showers mid-May–mid-October; state park permit required ($35 annual, $7 daily).*

There's a wonderful dichotomy here. Split Rock is one of the most visited places in the state of Minnesota, but its camping area is one of the quietest and most secluded of any state park. It was an easy choice for our top pick.

Notice I didn't say "campground"—because there isn't one, per se. Campers park in a central lot and tote their gear, using provided two-wheel carts, to campsites that are anywhere from about a hundred yards to 0.3 mile from the lot, and seldom in view of each other. It's the perfect cross between car camping and backpacking;

■ Secluded site at Split Rock

no headlights shining into your tent at 2 a.m., but none of the deprivation that carrying your house on your back requires. (A shower building with indoor toilets and water is available just off the parking lot; it's open spring–fall.)

Half of the sites provide views of Lake Superior, and even the inland sites that don't are more secluded and picturesque than ones you'll find almost anywhere else.

If you're looking for a short jaunt from car to camp, try sites 2 or 3, but be aware that the Little Two Harbors Hiking Trail that passes in front of the sites does compromise privacy a little. On the other hand, these sites are closest to the park's pebble beach, where it's easy to loll away a few hours listening to the waves crash; they're also the closest sites to the lighthouse. Site 1 might be the best in the park, just a short walk from your car but off the trail; while you won't see the lake from your tent, just climb the little hill on the site and you'll find a bench that overlooks the lake with a stunning view of the lighthouse. Two favorite sites are 18 and 19, which require you to push your cart up a moderately steep hill, but your effort will be rewarded when you see the lake stretching out before you.

With only 20 cart-in sites, Split Rock reservations are hard to come by in summer, even on weekdays. You can make reservations up to a year in advance, and many people do. While cancellations sometimes allow you to grab a good site at the last minute, the best advice is to book as early as you can.

Directions From Two Harbors, continue north on MN 61 for about 20 miles. The state park/campground is on your right near mile marker 46.

BACKUP BASE CAMP

Gooseberry Falls State Park (Minnesota Department of Natural Resources)

3206 MN 61 E, Two Harbors; 218-595-7100; dnr.state.mn.us/state_parks. $17–$23/night for drive-in sites, 69 sites; 1 kayak site available only for persons traveling to the park, first come, first served; reservations required for drive-in sites; sites have picnic table, fire ring, grill, flush and vault toilets, water, hot showers mid-May–mid-October; state park permit required ($35 annual, $7 daily).

If Split Rock Lighthouse State Park were a music venue, it'd be a small, intimate theater. Gooseberry, on the other hand, would be a big boisterous stadium. Your preference will depend on what kind of experience you're looking for. Gooseberry's campground can be crowded, and in many spots there is little foliage to separate one site from another. Groups of campers can on occasion be a bit noisy, and you may have to dodge kids on their bikes as you drive through the campground. But if solitude and seclusion are not requirements, you can't get any closer to the North Shore's quintessential waterfalls (three sets of them) and river gorge, which are a must-visit for anyone heading up the North Shore. The park also has a spacious and inviting visitor center, with exhibits and a large shop.

Directions From Two Harbors, continue north on MN 61 for about 13 miles.

INDOOR LODGING

Cove Point Lodge *4614 MN 61, Beaver Bay; 218-226-3221; covepointlodge.com*

Cove Point Lodge stands out by providing luxury accommodations, both lodge rooms and cottages, with an authentic north woods vibe at a variety of price levels. (Go for a corner room if you can get it.) Special packages are available for hikers and bikers. For those interested in working off a big breakfast, take the hiking path from the hotel to the Superior Hiking Trail, which gives you access to the dramatic cliffs above the Beaver River and at Fault Line Ridge. Fine dining—creative but not fussy—is available in the lodge dining room, with pub fare at the adjacent Cove Point Crossing Bar & Grill. Best of all? All accommodations feature views of Lake Superior.

Split Rock River

Gooseberry Cabins *3044 E. Castle Danger Road, Two Harbors; 218-834-3873; gooseberrycabins.net*

Minnesotans know a classic resort when they see one, and Gooseberry Cabins fits the bill. Eight cabins, for small groups and large, face Lake Superior, and you can have a shoreline campfire to end a perfect day.

FALL COLORS

Touring for fall colors is a popular pastime in Minnesota. The colors can be amazing in all corners of the state, but watching the leaves turn on the North Shore is spectacular. The only downside? The only traffic jams you'll run into on the North Shore will be in September and into October.

What makes the North Shore fall color show particularly interesting is that it stretches out for so long. Inland trees—notably the sugar maples—turn earliest, sometimes by mid-September. But the aspens and birch that are closer to Lake Superior show peak colors a week or two later. Colors can be good through the middle of October.

Because campsites at the North Shore can be hard to come by in fall color season, you should plan your fall visit far in advance. That means guessing which weekend will provide the best color. In general, I will book a visit for the last weekend in September and hope for the best. On occasion, if the colors have not peaked when I'm there, I'll make another visit in October.

To see the colors, most visitors will take scenic byways that run off of MN 61 along the shore. Which byway you take will depend on the time of the color change and your own personal preferences, but you can get more information by visiting superiorbyways.com/routes.

To keep track of when colors are changing around the state, bookmark dnr.state.mn.us/fall_colors. The site is regularly updated with current and predicted color peaks.

HIKING ○

Split Rock River Loop (part of the Superior Hiking Trail) *5.1 miles*

OK, I'll admit this may be a pretty bold statement, but there's not much more you can ask from a hiking trail than what you'll find on Split Rock River Loop—gorgeous views, a variety of landscapes, and enough length (about 5 miles) and elevation to keep veteran hikers happy but not enough to scare off novices (but you will work up a sweat).

Directions From the wayside parking area on the inland side of MN 61 at mile marker 43.5 (about 2.5 miles south of Split Rock Lighthouse State Park), hike the spur trail for a half mile to the junction with the Superior Hiking Trail (SHT). Follow the SHT up the river's west side, where you will pass two campsites (these are free sites managed by the Superior Hiking Trail Association). At about 2.5 miles you'll cross the river on a bridge. As you head back down the east side of the river, you'll pass another pair of campsites. At 4.3 miles you'll hit the spur trail that leads back down to MN 61. When you approach the highway, turn right on the path back to the parking lot.

(Here's a fun challenge: See if you can spot the split rock on this trail that gives the loop and the lighthouse its name.)

It is possible to access this loop from your campsite in the state park, but it will add a bit over 2 miles, each way, to your hike.

The split rock

Split Rock River Wayside to Beaver Bay (part of the Superior Hiking Trail) *11.3 miles*

If you're looking for something to really test your abilities, this will do it. The trail will light the fire in your calves, with steep ascents and descents throughout. Most hikers will average about 2 miles per hour (or less) on this segment, but because it's so long, if you're going to hike slowly, you may want to go out a few miles and turn around at a designated time. Your effort will be rewarded, though, with breathtaking views of Lake Superior (as well as inland) along the numerous ridgelines. Christmas Tree Ridge and Fault Line Ridge are especially picturesque, with SHT campsites near both that are good spots for a rest or lunch break.

Don't worry if you arrive at a campsite for a break and find it occupied. Campsites on the SHT are meant to be shared—in fact, that's the rule. But even if it wasn't, SHT hikers and backpackers are by and large a very friendly bunch, and you'll find people more than happy to share the space.

> **Directions** The starting point is at the same wayside parking area as for the Split Rock River Loop, on the inland side of MN 61 at mile marker 43.5. The trailhead at the Beaver Bay end can be reached by turning inland from MN 61 near mile marker 51, onto Lake County Road 4 (Lax Lake Road). The trailhead is just short of a mile up the road, on the right side.

Because this is not a loop trail, if you do the entire 11.3 miles, you'll have to find a way to get back to your basecamp after your hike. Fortunately, there are a couple of options.

The **Superior Hiking Shuttle** (218-834-5511, superiorhikingshuttle.com) operates on a schedule that is available online. You can plan to arrive at your hiking terminus in time to meet the shuttle and take it back to your starting point. But that puts pressure on you to stay on course, and the last thing you want in the woods is to have to adhere to a specific schedule. Here's a better idea: drive to where you want to end your hike, leave your vehicle, and pick up the shuttle there. Take it to the other end, start your hike, and head back toward your vehicle on your own schedule.

You can also use **Harriet Quarles Transportation** (218-370-9164 or 218-387-1801). Quarles doesn't work on a fixed timetable, so she can accommodate individual schedules, but you will need to call her to check availability and make reservations.

ROAD BIKING ⊘

Not too many years ago, you were taking your life in your hands trying to bike along the narrow shoulder of MN 61 along the North Shore. Now, however, cyclists have the **Gitchi-Gami State Trail** (ggta.org), a nonmotorized paved recreational trail that meanders along the lake side of MN 61. Plans call for the trail to eventually span about 90 miles, but, due to funding difficulties, only 29 miles have been completed, and no significant new construction has taken place since 2013. The good news is that a 14-mile section of the trail is complete between Gooseberry Falls State Park and the town of Beaver Bay, with a spur trail running into Split Rock Lighthouse State Park. You want a scenic bike trail that doesn't cost you a dime to use? It doesn't get any better than this.

You can access the route at five designated trailheads along this segment: the lower level parking lot within Gooseberry Falls State Park, the present southwest terminus of the trail; the Gooseberry Falls visitor center; Twin Points wayside; Split Rock Lighthouse Visitor Center; and the Beaver River trailhead in Beaver Bay, the present northeast terminus of the trail segment. The trailheads at the visitor centers offer parking, restroom facilities, and drinking water. Restaurants, restroom facilities, and other amenities (including ice cream) are also available just off the trail in Beaver Bay.

■ On the Gitchi-Gami State Trail

While portions of the trail can be managed by any family member, there are some steep inclines and curves in places, particularly in and near the state parks.

A map of the Gitchi-Gami State Trail bike route can be found online at dnr.state .mn.us/maps/state_trails/gitchi_gami.pdf. An interactive map is also available at ggta .org/map.php.

PADDLING ⊗

The Minnesota Department of Natural Resources has established a Lake Superior water trail (dnr.state.mn.us/watertrails/lswt), intended primarily for kayakers, that can be accessed in Two Harbors' **Burlington Bay** (MN 61 mile marker 26) and goes to Beaver Bay (MN 61 mile marker 49.5) and beyond. While bays and inlets along the route allow for leisurely paddling in good weather, this is Lake Superior, the largest freshwater lake in the world by surface area, and conditions can get treacherous. This is not a place to climb into a kayak for the first time unless you're content staying close to shore in a protected area (such as where the paddleboarders would be).

For a map of the Lake Superior Water Trail between Two Harbors and the Caribou River, visit files.dnr.state.mn.us/maps/kayaking/lswt_map2.pdf.

■ Split Rock Lighthouse

RAINY DAY 😎

It's easy to speed through Two Harbors on the way to your North Shore destination, maybe stopping for gas or a quick burger, seeing nothing except what's along the 2-mile main drag. But if you're looking for activities when weather keeps you from serious outdoor exploration, the historic waterfront in Two Harbors is well worth a visit.

Lake County Historical Society campus *520 South Ave., Two Harbors; 218-834-4898; lakecountyhistoricalsociety.org/museums*

There's something for everyone here, including three museums:

The **Two Harbors Lighthouse Museum** features the oldest continuously operated lighthouse on the North Shore. Open Monday–Saturday 10 a.m.–6 p.m. and Sunday 10 a.m.–4 p.m.

The **Depot Museum** is the former headquarters of the Duluth and Iron Range Railroad and features exhibits on the railroad, iron mining, timber, and commercial fishing. Open Monday–Saturday 9 a.m.–5 p.m. and Sunday 10 a.m.–4 p.m.

The **3M/Dwan Museum,** birthplace of the company in 1902, is listed on the National Register of Historic Places. The museum pays homage to the early days of the company that became an international force in research and development (and invented the Post-It Note). Open Memorial Day–mid-October, Monday–Friday noon–5 p.m., Saturday 11 a.m.–5 p.m., and Sunday 11 a.m.–4 p.m.

Admission is $5 for each museum, or $10 per person for all three. Tickets are good for two days.

And farther up the shore, don't forget . . .

Split Rock Lighthouse *3713 Split Rock Lighthouse Road, Two Harbors; 218-226-6372; mnhs.org/splitrock*

It doesn't have to be a rainy day to visit the lighthouse, but with so many outdoor activities available, sometimes it takes a few drops of rain to make it rise to the top of the sightseeing list. You can visit parts of the lighthouse grounds and the gift shop for free, but if you really want the full scoop on one of Minnesota's iconic locations, you'll want to pay for admission to the site, which entitles you to an entertaining and informative tour of the lighthouse. Getting close to the lighthouse's glass lens is worth the price of admission.

Open daily, 10 a.m.–6 p.m., admission is $10 for adults and $6 for children (age 4 and under admitted free). The lighthouse and interiors of the historic buildings on the grounds are closed during the winter months.

FOOD AND DRINK 🍴

Rustic Inn Café *2773 MN 61, Two Harbors; 218- 834-2488; rusticinn.cafe*

I've been enjoying meals at the Rustic Inn for more than two decades, but because the place has been around for nearly a century, I guess I'm still a relative newcomer. The Rustic's longevity is well deserved. A breakfast skillet or pancakes at the Rustic have marked the end of many a camping or canoe trip, but at dinner time it's hard to resist the wild rice meatloaf. And while there may be other places on the North Shore better known for pies, the Rustic's are as good as any. Tip: Ask to sit in the smaller dining room off on the west side—it's part of the original building that came along when the place moved to a new location in the mid-1980s.

Vanilla Bean *812 7th Ave., Two Harbors; 218-834-3714; thevanillabean.com*

The Vanilla Bean can be easy to miss among the cluster of shops as you roll into Two Harbors, but it's definitely worth watching for. The Bean has stepped it up a notch since changing hands in 2014. I think it's the best coffee in town, and the walleye cakes are just one of the creative breakfasts on the menu. The Iron Ranger pasty is a solid dinner choice. They get extra points for offering some gluten-free choices.

Castle Danger Brewery *17 7th St., Two Harbors; 218-834-5800; castledangerbrewery.com*

Craft brewers may have become as common as mosquitoes in Minnesota, but as the inevitable shakeout takes place, Castle Danger (brewing since 2011) is standing the test of time. There's nothing very fancy about its taproom in downtown Two Harbors, just a selection of suds wide enough—and tasty enough—to satisfy any discerning beer drinker. The pet-friendly patio is a plus.

Camp 61 *1017 Main St., Beaver Bay; 218-226-4351; campsixtyone.com*

When Todd and Carol Krynski took over the old Inn at Beaver Bay in 2010, it was part of a fading stretch of tourist attractions along the village's main drag. They gave the block a jolt by renovating and rejuvenating the spot and opening Camp 61. The original pine walls remain, but most everything else has been refreshed, including the menu. There's plenty of traditional North Shore fare, such as Lake Superior herring, but Krynski's barbecue ribs may be the best in the area.

GEAR AND RESUPPLY 🛒

Harbor Kayak and Paddleboard Rental *MN 61 and Park Road (entrance to Burlington Bay Campground), Two Harbors; 218-393-4545*

Owners Melanie Mojkowski and Christie Higgins will rent you the gear you need, including kayaks and paddleboards, and can help you plot a route in Agate Bay or Burlington Bay that will match your capabilities. Open daily, 8 a.m.–8 p.m., weather permitting.

Spokengear *1130 11th Ave., Two Harbors; 218-834-2117; spokengear.com*

This small, independently owned shop offers bikes for sale or rent, accessories, repair, and advice. It also has a sister company in the same building, Cedar Coffee, where you can grab an espresso, breakfast, or lunch.

Granite Gear *2312 10th St., Two Harbors; 218-834-6157; granitegear.com*

If you're a hardcore gearhead—and it's OK to admit it if you are—you know that Granite Gear makes some of the finest backpacks and outdoor gear you can buy. But you may not know that the company has been headquartered in Two Harbors since 1986. Some of its products are made right here, including gear that is used by the Navy SEALs. While this may not be a full-service gear or resupply spot, you can buy packs and other Granite Gear products here, and get expert advice from the people who help make the stuff. The showroom is open Monday–Friday 9 a.m.–4:30 p.m.

Superior Hiking Trail Association *731 7th Ave., Two Harbors; 218-834-2700*

Anyone who is going to set foot on the Superior Hiking Trail (and why would you be on the North Shore if you aren't?) would benefit from a quick stop at the office of the organization that is in charge of the trail. Besides picking up maps, books, or SHT-themed gear, you can find out the latest trail conditions from the people who know every inch of it. This should probably be your first stop on the way to your destination. Hours vary, so call to check.

Take a break and listen to the waves at Split Rock's pebble beach.

ADDITIONAL RESOURCES

BIKING 🔧

dot.state.mn.us/bike/maps *Routes and maps for US bike trails in Minnesota, as well as county bike maps that can be downloaded as PDFs*

dnr.state.mn.us/state_parks/starter_kit/wheels.html *A comprehensive listing of paved, unpaved, and singletrack trails under the jurisdiction of the Minnesota Department of Natural Resources*

havefunbiking.com *Guides, maps, and articles on road and trail riding in Minnesota for the novice to the seasoned cyclist*

metrobiketrails.weebly.com *A guide to more than 70 bike trails in the five-county Minneapolis–Saint Paul metro area*

mnbiketrailnavigator.blogspot.com *Offers a comprehensive schedule of bike tours, rides, races, and events, as well as links to bike maps throughout the state*

morcmtb.org *The website of Minnesota Off-Road Cyclists, which maintains more than 100 miles of singletrack in the Twin Cities area*

singletracks.com/minnesota-bike-trails_23.html *Reviews, ratings, and trail conditions of mountain bike trails in Minnesota*

CAMPING

Best Tent Camping: Minnesota by Tom Watson *Descriptions and reviews of 50 private, state park, and state and national forest campgrounds in Minnesota. Includes color maps, driving directions, and GPS coordinates.*

Best Minnesota Camper Cabins: Roughing It in Comfort by Tom Watson *A book for anyone who wants to sleep in the woods but not in a tent—an overview of the camper cabins offered in Minnesota state parks*

Camping the North Shore by Andrew Slade *Recreational opportunities on Minnesota's North Shore, focusing on 23 campgrounds in the Lake Superior region*

CLIMBING 🖊

mountainproject.com/area/105812481/minnesota *Links to climbing routes in Minnesota, as well as climbing gyms and indoor walls and reviews of classic routes*

HIKING 🥾

Hiking the North Shore by Andrew Slade *A listing of 50 day hikes, from 2 to 12 miles long, in the state parks and state and national forests along Minnesota's North Shore*

Hiking Waterfalls in Minnesota by Steve Johnson *Descriptions, maps, and color photos for hikes that lead to nearly 100 waterfalls in the state, in popular city parks as well as secluded areas*

60 Hikes Within 60 Miles: Minneapolis and Saint Paul by Tom Watson *Fourth edition, offers detailed descriptions of hiking opportunities within 60 miles of the Twin Cities*

americanhiking.org *The American Hiking Society advocates for the preservation of natural areas, including hiking trails. The website lists hiking trails in Minnesota and other states.*

dnr.state.mn.us/hiking *Links to lists of Minnesota hiking trails in state parks, forests, and other natural areas*

hikingproject.com *Trail information, including interactive maps, route options, elevation charts, photos, ratings, and local events*

traillink.com *Website and app provide detailed descriptions and maps of hiking trails, along with reviews and photos. Site requires free registration.*

PADDLING ✖

bwca.com *Website devoted to the Boundary Waters Canoe Area Wilderness, including planning tools, trip reports, maps, entry point descriptions, and forums*

mncanoe.org *The Minnesota Canoe Association website lists links to paddling organizations, plus event calendars, news, and forums.*

paddling.com *Comprehensive paddling location maps, plus gear information, reviews, and message boards*

threeriversparks.org/activity/paddling *Paddling opportunities in the west suburban Minneapolis–Saint Paul area, which includes 27,000 acres of parks and trails*

GENERAL INFORMATION

exploreminnesota.com *The state's tourism promotion agency offers personalized suggestions for outdoor activities in Minnesota, as well as suggestions for lodging, dining, events, and travel.*

mn.gov/greatoutdoors *Features search tools to locate Minnesota parks and trails*

mnrovers.org *Minnesota Rovers Outdoor Club is a nonprofit organization that offers outdoor adventures every week of the year, including hiking, backpacking, biking, canoeing, kayaking, snowshoeing, cross-country skiing, and rock climbing.*

startribune.com/sports/outdoors *Weekly newspaper section devoted to coverage of the outdoors in Minnesota, including news and features about camping, backpacking, bicycling, paddling, and running*

INDEX

Check out this great title from
— Adventure Publications! —

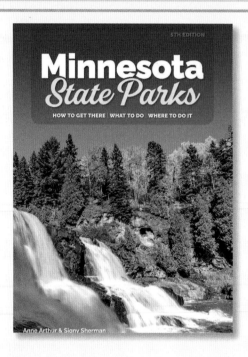

Minnesota State Parks

by Anne Authur and Signy Sherman   6 x 8.5, paperback
ISBN: 978-1-64755-250-3   328 pages
$22.95, 5th Edition   Color photographs, maps, index

When you consider a visit to Minnesota's state parks, you might imagine hiking, bicycling, camping, fishing, swimming, bird-watching, or simply relaxing beside a babbling river. Of course, you're right. The beautiful parks are perfect escapes for your favorite outdoor activities—but there's so much more to do. Minnesota's state parks offer a multitude of unique experiences and new adventures! Discover them all in *Minnesota State Parks* by Anne Arthur and debut author Signy Sherman.

This comprehensive guide spotlights all 75 state parks and state recreation areas in the Land of 10,000 Lakes. Each entry includes full-color photography, a map, and the details you want to know—including a park overview and descriptions of the trails, campgrounds, and interpretive programs. Plus, the authors' tips help to ensure that you maximize the fun.

The Story of AdventureKEEN

We are an independent nature and outdoor activity publisher. Our founding dates back more than 40 years, guided then and now by our love of being in the woods and on the water, by our passion for reading and books, and by the sense of wonder and discovery made possible by spending time recreating outdoors in beautiful places.

It is our mission to share that wonder and fun with our readers, especially with those who haven't yet experienced all the physical and mental health benefits that nature and outdoor activity can bring.

In addition, we strive to teach about responsible recreation so that the natural resources and habitats we cherish and rely upon will be available for future generations.

We are a small team deeply rooted in the places where we live and work. We have been shaped by our communities of origin—primarily Birmingham, Alabama; Cincinnati, Ohio; and the northern suburbs of Minneapolis, Minnesota. Drawing on the decades of experience of our staff and our awareness of the industry, the marketplace, and the world at large, we have shaped a unique vision and mission for a company that serves our readers and authors.

We hope to meet you out on the trail someday.

#bewellbeoutdoors

ABOUT THE AUTHOR

photographed by Allyson Moravec

Jeff Moravec has spent more than 30 years (and nearly 500 nights in a tent) exploring the outdoors in Minnesota. In pursuing outdoor adventures—including hiking, backpacking, camping, biking, and paddling—he has criss-crossed Minnesota, from the North Shore of Lake Superior and the Boundary Waters Canoe Area to the tallgrass prairie and blufflands in the state's southern region. An accomplished writer and wildlife photographer, Jeff regularly recounts his travels in the Outdoors Weekend section of Minneapolis's *Star Tribune*. His writings have also appeared in national publications, and his photos have been displayed throughout the Midwest. Jeff has also written about and photographed the northern lights in Iceland; the lions of the Serengeti (Tanzania, Africa); and the windswept shorelines of Scotland and Ireland. Jeff has also spent decades as a volunteer for the Superior Hiking Trail Association and other outdoors organizations in Minnesota, working to protect, maintain, and improve the state's natural resources.